THE TROUBLE WITH BEING HUMAN

The Trouble with Being Human

EUGENE KENNEDY

Originally published under the title
THE TROUBLE BOOK

IMAGE BOOKS
A Division of Doubleday & Company, Inc.
Garden City, New York
1986

Image Books edition published February 1986
by special arrangement with The Thomas More Press.

Library of Congress Cataloging-in-Publication Data
Kennedy, Eugene C.
The trouble with being human.
Reprint. Originally published: The trouble book.
Chicago: T. More Press, c1976.
1. Conduct of life. 2. Adjustment (Psychology)
I. Title.
[BF637.C5K462 1986] 158'.2 85-13178
ISBN 0-385-23239-X (pbk.)

F.S.

CONTENTS

THE TROUBLE WITH BEING HUMAN

1

And Lie Down to Peaceful Dreams . . .

We would all like to close our eyes every night and dream of peaceful and beautiful scenes, of uninterrupted friendship, of good times and fair weather, of sailing at high noon with full sails toward warm water and white beaches. But such are the hydraulics of the human situation that dragons often rise out of the blackened night and monsters streaming spume scatter the tide as they charge our boat. We are restless and the sun refuses to set on our day's activities even though the moon has long ago risen in the night sky. We cannot shake loose from the associations of the day as they transform themselves and deny us sleep. Or visions we cannot bear to look at loom up from sources that seem totally alien to us. Who is this person we discover in the hours before dawn, this peace-loving individual blinking away the ghosts of uneasy dreams? How often we resemble the character in *Play It As It Lays,* who, after driving the California freeways all day, lies in bed watching the flashing of the unending parade of cars on the ceiling, bringing the long day back into night.

A night's quiet rest does not seem too much to ask, or just a e of worries, one whole day without a sign or an anxious eling, twenty-four hours without regrets or misgivings. But these do not always come easily, not even to the most innocent among us. That is why sleeping pills are so popular, why cocktail hours are not likely to disappear, why friends can feel an urgent need for closeness at odd hours. Human beings are wired sensitively into the current of life. They pick up signals all the time, whether they know it or not, not like dead letters stacking up in an airless post office, but as resonating messages in their living souls. We are what we experience.

That makes the journey through those quiet meadows into that old-fashioned town where everyone works hard, tells the truth, and sleeps soundly until the cock crows against a dazzling blue sky something more for the movies than for real life. Ours is fundamentally an uneasy condition. The sooner we realize this the less we will be disturbed by twinges of the spirit. We are not wax dummies nor are we designed to maintain a coolness that amounts to indifference in the face of life's assorted fortunes. We constantly act and react and our best stance is always a somewhat precarious balance. Our trouble lies in expecting ourselves to be different, in thinking that we should never be anxious or have strange fantasies, or feel things go bump in our souls in the middle of the night.

We are not characters in a Walt Disney movie smiling and thinking beautiful thoughts all the time. We are like boats, more at home in the never-quiet sea than we would be wedged like a rock into a stable landscape. Tied to a dock, ships feel the pull of deep and distant tides; even at anchor they ride the strange and powerful sea. Although it is one of the delusions of history, human beings are not made to be at rest any more than boats are. It is in their nature to be responsive, to match the movement of the wind and water, and so are we. There are very few moments of total inactivity that fit the nature or the needs of human personality. People are killed by blood vessels that clog like a can of fat in a refrigerator when they are inactive. The heart is a muscle that thrives on exercise the way the human spirit does on giving itself away. The case for contentment consisting in the great American Zonk-Out in front of the television set cannot be taken seriously. We are meant to be involved in life intensely and on many levels. That is what is good for us.

Living deeply, however, has dangerous side effects. Persons cannot invest themselves in relationships with others, for example, and think that they will never be hurt, have misgivings, or make mistakes. And we feel all of these down deep, in the tensed coils of the soul that unravel noisily after we have gone to bed. The nightly lighting of our inner world is one of the proofs that we are alive and well in the human situation. We are forever in harm's way; something is always happening to us, even when we are accomplishing purposeful things, that puts a surcharge on our energy reserves and leaves some kind of mark on the inside of our souls. We simply cannot feel deeply about life and not hear inside ourselves the constant echoes of our experience. Living and loving persons are always in trouble of one kind or another. That is a vital sign never noted on hospital charts but just as important as breathing and blood pressure.

People who try to eliminate trouble from life only guarantee that they will pile up plenty of unnecessary woes. An important distinction exists between the troubles we can't live without and the superfluous troubles we should be able to do without. There is enough trouble in leading a steady and purposeful life; enough trouble even for healthy people involved in growing, caring, and letting people be. Trouble enough are all such things and we do not need the unnecessary troubles that we stack up like sandbags on our souls when we are untruthful, underconfident, or too filled with fear. We frequently have a lot to do with fashioning the strands of our own unrest. To be able to separate necessary from unnecessary trouble is a big step toward handling all of life more effectively.

For example, some persons view life as a kind of illness in itself. They are intimidated by the shortcomings of the human situation, made desperate, for example, by the inevitability of aging or the waning of their powers or influence. They seek a cure for life or they seek treatments that will spare them the price of human existence. They would march into eternity with

... never wrinkled by worry or surprise, with hands still smooth and innocent of work. They want to outwit life, finding the latest and most perfect way to be in style, exerting themselves enormously to achieve the prescribed expertise in everything from sexuality to apartment decorating. But, worst of all worlds, they never do get it quite right, or it all keeps changing on them, and they have to set out in a whole new direction every few months. They are permanently anxious, frequently exhausted, and almost always without the peaceful dreams they desire so much. They may manage to snare some fleeting contentment but they never catch up with lasting happiness.

Life cannot be managed like pneumonia or some other disease. It demands to be understood rather than treated. We must enter into it, understanding and accepting the terms of our relationship with it, neither demanding too much nor settling for too little. And the best way to approach this is through a realistic appreciation and acceptance of what it means to be human. It is as simple and as awesome as that.

It helps, for example, to realize that we are always living on top of our own history, on top of the spirits and genes of our ancestors. We have not emerged from nowhere; we are not without our personal and collective histories. We do not understand the complexity of our inheritance nor the subtlety of our social learning. But there is a lot there that has come out of our past, both remote and immediate. We may not be able to sort it all out but we can feel its enormous power. We are not strangers on the earth. We come from tribes and traditions, all of which have left their imprint on our spirit.

We ride the great tide of our own unconscious selves. We do not fully understand the sudden shifts and churning inside of us. Nor can we find a name for the moods that may settle like a druid spell on us. Where does it all come from if not from within us? There is literally more to us than meets the eye and the person who looks only at the surface behavior of humankind misses the richest, deepest, and most powerful parts of it.

And it is not all bad. We have dark corners, that is true, and a talent for evil with which we must come to terms. The forces of the unconscious, however, are not foreign matter. They are, in a clumsy phrase, us. It is good to recognize this and to get acquainted with this infinitely complex aspect of our personalities. Our most creative intuitions may spring from it; so too may our darkest dreams.

The unconscious is that mass of living psychological filaments where all our experience is stored; it is more than a storeroom, however, because it has a life of its own, a shadow life closely connected with what we feel we are aware of, affecting us deeply, reacting silently, sending up symbols like bubbles from its own depths. We may deceive ourselves on the surface but what truly happens to us in life is accurately recorded at the unconscious levels of personality. And from this energy source we erect the barriers called defenses against conscious knowledge. We are ever active on all levels of our being, forging pacts with eros, making compromises with reality, traveling without the usual limitations of time. An astonishing place indeed!

In the unconscious we experience the deep conflicts that we cannot face in our conscious lives. They make their way toward the light of awareness in distorted forms; they can make it seem that demons lurk in our depths. We are startled and puzzled by the symptoms or groups of symptoms, the only evidence of unconscious conflicts that we usually see. Persons may, for example, develop a fear of heights or a psychosomatic illness. They see and are vexed by the external problems but the roots run down deep in the dynamic unconscious. Without some grasp of the reality of these unconscious processes and their role in our lives we can only be astounded and bewildered by our troubles. We may look for magical explanations, search the stars for a sign, have our tea leaves read, or make our decisions by the cut of the cards. One is as good as the other when we fail to appreciate the unconscious side of ourselves.

We deal more effectively with the necessary troubles of life when we have a feeling for our complexity, for the dynamic nature of existence, for the surging energies that lie beneath our conscious life. There is no rest when such powerful forces are an intimate part of our own experience all the time. There is only the steady effort to keep up with ourselves and the many layers of our reactions. It is enough to make us puff with exertion. But that is one of the necessary problems of life. Give up on listening to ourselves and we give up on life itself. We don't live trying to keep up with the Joneses nearly as much as we do in trying to keep up with ourselves.

But listening to—being surprised by and sometimes dumbfounded at—the far reaches of our own inner experience allows us to deal in a healthy and open manner with life. We can do this on mutually agreeable terms and even enjoy the excitement of being a complicated, reacting, and very alive human person. The peaceful dreams start to come when we understand that.

Samples and Examples

The unconscious as it has been discussed in this chapter has been part of the American culture for some time now. It is something we ought to get to know more about. It is not going to go away. We will, in fact, hear from it regularly. So we might as well get to recognize and respect it, not as an alien force bent on pushing us over the edge of sanity or adjustment but as something that is a profound part of our identity. When we appreciate the unconscious as an almost breathing aspect of our personalities we can take it into account, understand ourselves and our own actions better, deal more constructively with the problems and difficulties of life and also react and deal with those around us more positively. What is the unconscious like and what should we recognize about ourselves in view of its living presence with us throughout our lives?

People are always trying to tell the truth about themselves. If we remember this simple principle, applying it generously even to ourselves, we will be well ahead of the game in working through the problems of our existence. It is the unconscious side of our lives that is always trying to get through to the outside world and to express what the truth about ourselves really is. We have a powerful force, in other words, trying to manifest both to us and to all those around us what we are really like. If we listen to it we will learn a great deal. It may seem to contradict what we hold consciously, but if we are patient and listen long and carefully enough we will see the wisdom of the total personality in action. This kind of wisdom surpasses the rational exercises of the mind alone.

We tell the truth, however, in a special language. That is why it is worth deepening our appreciation of the unconscious. The truth comes out sideways and backwards and in negatives, in symbolic gestures, in things we forget to do, in those slips of the tongue, and in the overall pattern or design of our lives and activities.

We may, for example, publicly say the very opposite from what is true of us but we give many clues at the same time, either by the excessive emotion attached to our statement or through the gestures by which we try to take it back even as we utter it; these make our meaning clear. And these are generally graphically clear signals. They are clearly present and they are not sent from some place outside ourselves. They emerge from our own personalities. The truth will out and if we can attune ourselves to the way we regularly try to tell ourselves the truth about ourselves we will avoid a lot of unnecessary trouble. All we have to do is listen and look carefully.

Some aspects of the unconscious that are important to recognize include the following:

(1) *It is a living if hidden dimension of personality.* It is powerful and it demands our respect and attention because it goes on functioning whether we attend consciously to it or not. It asserts itself if we neglect its messages or try to go against them or write off its content as irrelevant to our lives. The unconscious gets out—in troubled forms occasionally—when we are not open to what it expresses about us. We can save a lot of trouble, then, by our willingness to listen to what is so much a part of ourselves. We invite trouble when we will not do this.

(2) *The unconscious is a timeless place.* It is difficult for us to imagine the world without time. We are so caught up in the pressure of deadlines and we are sometimes so afraid of the

passage of time that the very concept of an environment in which this no longer has any relevance is almost impossible to understand. But there is no past and there is no future in the unconscious. It is all there all at once. There is nothing of our experience that is lost and what seems chronologically to have happened years ago is as fresh as a spring flower in the unconscious. It is always just occurring. That is why events from childhood retain their power over our behavior even when we can no longer recall them easily in our own awareness.

(3) *There is no negative in the unconscious.* There is no way, in other words, to say *no* or *not.* When conscious negatives are excessively insisted on, we may suspect that the unconscious truth is different. We can safely discard the *noes* and *nots.* We know that the real meaning of what we vehemently deny is just the opposite. It is impossible to understand ourselves unless we accept this profound truth. When we find, as mentioned before, that we are insisting on something a great deal we may catch ourselves on the edge of an unconscious defense—the snag of denial. We may not understand why we are doing it, but too much insistence, for example, that we are not jealous, that we are not upset, that we are not this way or that, is firsthand evidence that we probably *are* that way and that we are not allowing ourselves to look at it.

Different Kinds of Trouble

In this chapter we talk about *necessary* and *unnecessary* trouble. It is time to distinguish between them and to give examples of each.

Necessary trouble may loosely be defined as the pain and struggle—the inevitable discomfort—that is connected with anything that brings us more to life. There is some pain involved in any experience that truly enlarges us, that enables us to be a fuller, richer presence in life. We can tell when we have become more of ourselves; there is usually some kind of trouble involved—some hard truths we must face, something we have to let go of—involved in this experience. Necessary trouble does not take life away from us. It may cause us to suffer but it does not destroy us or lessen us in any way. Neither does it destroy or lessen those around us.

Some examples of the *necessary trouble* of existence include the following:

(1) *Living the truth of our existence.* That, of course, is the problem of life. It means living by principle, living from inside rather than from out, and pushing always toward what is genuine about us. That is what produces maturity, but we have to do the struggling for ourselves. If we listen to ourselves, if we care to hear, we can discover that truth. It is a necessary trouble for a full life.

(2) *Being faithful*—a concept many people have found troublesome—is also a necessary aspect of the fulfilling human struggle. That includes being faithful to ourselves, to our words, and to our spouses. There is a long list of things that are worth being faithful to and the list of things that may justify breaking faith is very short indeed. It may even be nonexistent. Infidelity, unfortunately, has had a run of popularity as a principle rather than just as an accidental occurrence in the life of contemporary persons. But infidelity, besides being a lot of unnecessary trouble, deprives people of the experience of their own fullness that is vital to their existence and development as human persons. It is worth thinking about, if only because so many people write it off. Down deep, however, most good people recognize that being faithful may be a struggle but that it is not to be underrated.

(3) *Being sensitive to the feelings of others.* This is a very troublesome but necessary thing if we want to survive as loving human beings. There is no substitute for it. Most of us, of course, think that it is other people who should be sensitive to our feelings. What we find, however, is that if we take the trouble to be aware of and treat respectfully the emotional lives of others, others treat us in the same way. We get what we give out in this department.

(4) *Taking a stand.* Not everybody has to be a Thomas More in order to take a stand on an important issue. We take stands all

the time, as a matter of fact, or we make ourselves sound like we take a stand. That is a favorite trick of politicians trying to keep themselves out of trouble with their voters. Perceptive voters, however, don't care for that treatment. Double-talk is far more trouble than taking an honest stand after we have searched ourselves and our convictions with honesty and integrity. This need not be on a world-shaking issue of conscience. Any issue which involves our conscience, however, is vitally important to our integrity as human beings. You can't take a stand if you don't believe in anything. Neither can you take a stand if you believe in everything. We have to take the trouble to find out what we believe in and why, if we are going to make this an intelligent part of our lives.

(5) *Almost anything connected with love and friendship is a lot of trouble.* The rewards are very high, of course, but some people want these without going through the trouble always connected with them. Their special troubles, most of them centering on becoming less selfish, attach to learning the meaning of friendship and love. These include taking the time to be understanding—which is something that cannot be faked. It takes time and trouble to be able to forgive somebody and to try to be ready to forget. There is trouble involved in cleansing ourselves of the grudges we can sometimes so willingly hold against those who have offended us. There is trouble involved in letting other people do things for us, in allowing ourselves, in other words, to be dependent in a healthy way in certain relationships. No love survives very long if one or the other partner is always giving and never lets the other reciprocate. Love thrives on healthy reciprocity. A corollary of this is involved in allowing ourselves to be forgiven by others. There is a special quality to the existential mystery of forgiving and being forgiven. Sometimes we are better at one side of it than we are at the other. There is trouble, even if it is only a little self-consciousness, connected with letting other people forgive us for our offenses against them. It is trouble worth taking if we want to sleep well, however.

Unnecessary Troubles

We could all make our own long list of the unnecessary troubles in life because we all have firsthand knowledge of them. We have also had a lot of other people telling us what is wrong with us; friends and relatives willing and sometimes anxious to point out our mistakes. We do not lack for editors as far as living goes. All we have to do is pick and sort out the things that have caused us the most trouble and given us the least advantage and we will know well what to avoid in order to have a happier life. The difficulty may sometimes lie in the fact that we seldom do something as simple as that. We do not like to think about the things that hurt us. We would rather look away or rationalize them in some fashion. It is a necessary trouble, however, to find the truth about the way we produce unnecessary troubles for ourselves.

The following is a loose definition of this pervasive phenomenon: Any activities we could do something about if we wanted to that we let diminish our lives or the lives of those close to us. This does not mean activities that literally kill other people. We can cripple others invisibly; we can lessen or deny the chance for a fuller life both to others and to ourselves. These come under the heading of *unnecessary trouble.* These include the following:

(1) *The troubles we pile up for ourselves when we try to avoid trouble.* There is a great deal of unnecessary psychic energy expended in trying to avoid the ordinary troubles and difficulties of life. These efforts are only successful in the short term anyway and they are frequently exhausting. When they are successful they make it impossible for us to experience some of the things that are essential for our identity as human beings. Persons, for example, who avoid involvement with other people in order to avoid having their feelings hurt also rule real friendship and love out of life. That is a lot of unnecessary trouble. We frequently get into this by trying to use shortcuts the way a student tries to patch a new term paper together out of pieces of several

old papers. The amount of labor and wit involved in this undertaking could produce three brand-new term papers.

(2) *Unnecessary trouble is found in any of those things we do for vain and superficial reasons.* This includes the great pains we go to to impress other persons, to look good, or in order to get the attention of others. Sometimes these complicated efforts do work and the involved trouble can seem justified even though it is unnecessary. All too often, however, those troublesome efforts do not work. We find out that nobody was looking at us or listening to us; it was all for naught. How much struggle has been involved in similar vain undertakings!

(3) *Unnecessary trouble is associated with the things we do to prove that we are important, impressive, or that we are adults.* Troubles multiply whenever we put a lot of effort into proving something that, in the long run, cannot ever be proved. Strenuous efforts that go into proving masculinity or femininity always contain the edge of an unconscious message about inner uncertainties. The world has grown wise enough to recognize this but many individuals have not yet learned to avoid all the unnecessary troubles that go with demonstrating what they can never prove satisfactorily anyway.

(4) *Unnecessary trouble clusters around our many efforts to escape conflicts, obligations, or difficult situations in which we feel we will be embarrassed.* Sometimes people get themselves involved in very serious trouble—far more trouble than the situation they are trying to avoid—because they cannot overcome some small fear or uncertainty or shyness with others. They trace circuitous routes through existence, avoiding possible friends and good times, denying themselves legitimate pleasures in order to avoid, for example, the social unease they would feel on certain occasions. They miss a lot that they could enjoy and they experience enormous unnecessary trouble at the same time.

(5) *Untold trouble is connected with trying to be perfect.* There may not be anything that generates more unnecessary trouble than this strange imperative that seems to afflict every generation of human beings. People who strive to find the right combination, cover all the moves on the chessboard, or to find themselves

always fully and accurately accounted for sentence themselves to an extraordinary amount of superfluous difficulty. There is a second cousin to this problem: *Expecting other people to be perfect.* This leads us to be hard on them, to cause them conflicts, denying both to us and to them the easier and more rewarding relationship that is built on a sense of compassion about life.

(6) *Self-defeating behaviors of all varieties involve us in unnecessary trouble.* These include smoking, eating, or drinking too much. They include strange tactics in human relationships in which persons end up destroying friendship whenever it becomes too close or too demanding for them. Self-defeats abound but they are not lightning bolts from the fates. They issue from human beings themselves. The question that helps people to understand this unnecessary trouble comes to this: *What are we getting out of doing these things to ourselves?* This can put us on the road to understanding the strange design we have introduced into our life and can help us to free ourselves from it.

(7) *Closely related to this is enjoying unnecessary and self-punishing guilt.* Many people seem to relish feeling guilty. They like to be punished for deeds and misdeeds about which they are not quite clear but about which they feel quite uneasy. They cannot get through the day without a dose of self-punishing guilt. This particular brand of unnecessary trouble has ruined the lives of many persons.

(8) *Closely related to this is the unnecessary trouble of making others feel guilty,* one of the extraordinary achievements of the heavily neurotic. This is one of the dirtiest of the dirty tricks because it is a prize manipulation that may in fact control people for a long while. In the long run, however, it is destructive both for those who experience it and for those who inflict it on others. They get caught up in a crusted web of guilt and can no longer free themselves.

(9) *There is unnecessary trouble in settling for what is adolescent in ourselves.* We can achieve some perspective from which we can identify the things that are healthy and the things that are unhealthy in our personality. When we settle for things that come out on a lesser level of development than that of which we are

capable, then we involve ourselves in many unnecessary difficulties. When we indulge, for example, our daydreaming or our self-glorification; when we put on a show to get attention and end up losing the respect of others, we settle for what is adolescent about us. Anybody can make a long list of these.

(10) *The greatest of unnecessary troubles comes when fear is our motive in carrying out the activities of our lives.* We never can outwit this fear. We can, however, be deceived and undone by it regularly. When fear reigns we are always looking over our shoulders, we are always suspicious, and we can never rest or live in a peaceful kind of way. Closely related to this is living our lives in order to meet the expectations of other persons. This does not leave much room for a genuine experience or expression of ourselves. It causes us to spend a lot of time and effort developing techniques to win or wheedle our way into the good graces of other persons. It is all built on a shaky foundation, however, and persons who live life on this basis can never comfortably turn their back on the world that at any moment may suddenly withdraw its approval.

There is enough necessary trouble connected with living to convince us to avoid the unnecessary troubles!

2

Start at the End

Most people—even if they are unwilling to admit it—find themselves fascinating. We let the truth out, of course, by our willingness to let the topic of conversation shift to us without much protest. In many conversations we sit by daydreaming until we can break in to speak about our own exploits and accomplishments. We are always ready to tell the same old story, the one we have come to be known for, the one in which we have gradually shifted from a bystander to a central figure—and we get more heroic or prescient with each telling.

Sadly enough, we hardly pay sufficient attention to notice even that much about the way we make our way through everyday life. We are interested in ourselves more to get attention from others than to unlock any treasure of self-knowledge. And when we do seek such knowledge we frequently start at the wrong end of things; we also use the wrong technique to discover the truth about our own existence. In the first instance we try to plumb our deepest motives, and these are totally inaccessible to us. We want the final answer first. Secondly, we tend to think and talk about ourselves as though the problem of understanding human personality were a purely rational one. As a matter of fact, talking about ourselves sometimes makes it more difficult for us to penetrate deeper layers of our being. That is because talking lends itself to intellectualizing or abstracting ourselves from our emotions. That style of maneuver tends to keep us on the outside; it may produce the illusion but it does not deliver the substance of self-knowledge.

We might, then, skip the beginning of our woes for the moment. We know that the unconscious is there, bristling with the history of our lives. It does not, however, yield its secrets to us just because we want it to. Just as a flower need not be uprooted in order for us to begin to understand it, neither do we. We can begin at the end, asking ourselves not *why* we do things but what *are* the things that we do. We can attend to our own behavior, realizing that it is not accidental and that, if we try to understand it, it tells us a great deal about ourselves and the nature of our problems. We need to ask the first question rather than demand the final answer. What can we see, in other words, even if we do not fully understand it? We are, in fact, much more interesting than we might at first suspect. One of the languages we speak to ourselves all the time is that of our own actions; they are a rich and continuing source of self-revelation. We find much of the truth, not by looking in dark corners, but by looking at what we do in the light of day.

An example will help us to appreciate this. The husband greets his wife in the kitchen early in the morning with the following sentence: "Why don't you go upstairs and comb your hair? You don't look good that way." The wife reacts somewhat hostilely but she may not be able to admit to herself that this kind of "order" irritates her. The reaction is there below the level of consciousness even though she does not verbalize it. What does she do? That is, indeed, the question. She leaves the kitchen, but instead of going directly to the bedroom again to comb her hair she stops first to open the front door and then goes upstairs. The symbol is simple and clear. The conflict within her occasioned by her husband's order is symbolized by the fact that she first does something different—something she hadn't planned to do at all—than what he told her to do. She symbolizes defiance, irritation, and determination to do things as she decides to do them rather than as an immediate compliance to his wishes. A great deal, in other words, is caught up in that simple activity that takes but a few seconds to do. It is easier for her to comb her hair because she has already done something about her feelings by opening the front door. Such things happen dozens of times during anybody's daytime. They are filled with information. We do not usually try to interpret them; we just know that we feel better after we have performed such symbolic actions.

So we begin at the end and we are surprised at all that we can discover about ourselves. One of the things we instantly uncover is what a long process growing up really is. We are engaged in it all the time, working on the finishing touches that are never totally complete. Because we are working at growing up all the time, whether we want to admit it or not, we should not be surprised to see the signs of growing up in our behavior. Nor should we be appalled by the fact that we can see traces of the adolescent or regressive in our activities. Those are all flashes that reveal something of our complexity and of the dynamic nature of our personalities.

What we do on the behavioral level is highly instructive. It tells us how we typically handle problems or troubles of various kinds. If, when faced with frustration, we characteristically throw a tantrum or make a scene it is clear that we have not really gotten very far beyond the preadolescent level, that we operate pretty much from that layer of development and that it comes out when the pressure is on. The capacity to be patient and to refrain from judgment, the willingness to listen to and to be able to control our emergent feelings—the fact that we stop for a moment—these are signals that we live at an adult level. That is reflected in behavior that is far more calm, inventive, and cooperative with others when a problem situation arises. Between these two poles there is a wide range of other possibilities. What we do is instructive and we can only profit from watching ourselves closely in order to make out the signals we are constantly sending about who we are and what stage of growth we have reached. Beginning at the end leads us to our real selves.

There is, in fact, a moral question involved in paying close attention to ourselves. It is so easy to look away or to rationalize our behavior or never even to ask a curious question about ourselves. Such approaches prevent us from developing a moral sense at all. One of the first attributes of a well-developed moral sense is a willingness to take our own personalities seriously, that is, to try to see ourselves whole and to understand that, as we observe ourselves in actions, we begin to appreciate just who we are, what we look for in ourselves and others, and whether we are builders or destroyers of life. Our style reveals whether we respect our own personalities and how we use them in dealing with other persons. The pattern of morality can only be discerned through examination of our general way of treating ourselves and others in life. Watching what we do tells us a great deal about the level of our moral development.

We can observe whether we are coping with the challenges of life in an adult manner or whether there is always some loss involved, some harm to ourselves and to those close to us, whenever a point of choice or decision confronts us. Watching what we do also helps us to decide whether we may need some outside assistance in order to develop better insights into and therefore more certain control of our own behavior. Watching what we do gets us acquainted with ourselves from another viewpoint. It does not make us distant observers of our activities but rather offers us the opportunity for a new appreciation of our personal style.

What we observe in our behavior is sometimes a set of symptoms that we would like to get rid of. We may observe a syndrome that is neurotic, a phobia, for example, that interferes with our life and our work in a notable way. This does not mean that we have to get friendly with the neurotic aspects of our personalities. It does suggest, however, that we can at least recognize our neurosis. We can open diplomatic relations with it. Many people manage their troubles better when they can admit without fainting that there are aspects of their behavior that can be classified as neurotic, that there are, in other words, psychological processes at work which strongly affect and give shape to their external behavior. The things that they do are the outer signs—the special language—that is rooted in the unconscious conflicts to which they cannot address themselves directly. These behaviors are then no longer a total mystery nor a source of frustration to them because they can identify certain urges, obsessions, or other disturbing psychological events as part of what is not fully grown about themselves. We don't have to give full reign to our neurotic urges in order to acknowledge them and make room for them in our general consideration of ourselves. That gives us a fuller sense of our complex reality, enables us to be more patient and understanding, and frees us from the feeling that we are in the grip of alien forces.

It sometimes helps, in a nonpatronizing and nonself-pitying way, to acknowledge that there may be something sick about certain aspects of our personality. Nobody, of course, is supposed to use the word sick anymore. That is an inheritance, observers say, of the medical model which has had such an impact on the language of psychiatry. And yet neither the word sick nor the medical model is merited despite the barrage of criticism to which they have been subject in recent years. Why is this so? While those who emphasize the social learning characteristic of neurotic behavior may prefer us to use phrases that would reflect this, the medical model offers us an analogy with physical health that is both supportive and advantageous in dealing with our life difficulties. We know, for example, that in physical terms we may be called perfectly healthy—that we can pass any insurance examination in the world—and still suffer many symptoms of illness. We may, for example, have allergies, postnasal drip, trick knees, athlete's foot, headaches of one sort or another, and an agglomeration of other minor blemishes, itches, and twitches and still not be able to describe ourselves as unhealthy. These are the common ailments that go along with living. The organism is remarkable but it is not totally perfect nor does it function with the precision of the machine. There is always something dripping, functioning out of phase, or momentarily marring the picture of complete physical health. We can be healthy even though we are filled with the inevitable shortcomings and malfunctions of the human situation.

Psychologically we can recognize the same thing. We are not necessarily unhealthy because there are aspects of us that are not functioning properly. We live more comfortably with our imperfect selves when we can admit this and we stand up better against discouragement, not allowing ourselves to be destroyed when something unusual happens to us or when we find something surprising in our behavior. We don't have to indict the total personality, in other words, when these signals can be observed in our own activities. We can accept that there is part of us that is not functioning well, that is, in a certain sense, "sick" and we can still manage to live with it.

This is all part of what goes into establishing a healthy kind of relationship with our total selves. We are not just "thinking" or "intellectualizing" about ourselves. We possess a broader view than that which comes merely from rational analysis. We are open to the various levels of our experience and we try to translate accurately the various languages that we speak to ourselves all the time. We have a surer grip on our unity as human persons and we are less surprised at the diversity and complexity of what takes place within us.

The effects of this are twofold. We can accept ourselves more freely and we need not exist in a certain rigid way in our own eyes. When we function in this way we discover that we no longer need to be so defensive about ourselves. We can accept more and need to hide less. Secondly, the admission that there are certain aspects of us that are unfinished or "sick" enables us to make a better therapeutic alliance with what is strong and healthy in us. We do not have to look at ourselves as divided or picture ourselves at war within our personalities. We can, however, recognize what is adult and what is not about ourselves and we can bet wisely on following our strengths rather than our weaknesses. This is a way of taking one's existence seriously, of experiencing oneself in a new way, of being human toward oneself.

What can we conclude if we start at the end of our behavior and find that it leads us to a better general view of ourselves? First of all, we should never rush to judgment about our behavior. It is never quite so simple as we would like to think. There is always more to be learned and what we do cannot be cut off from our inner motivation. What we do becomes the starting point for tracing this behavior, for appreciating how it develops, and for taking these forces into account in the future.

Secondly, we realize that persons who want to manage life better do not focus simply on problems nor try only to solve these at the surface level. They start at the surface and make an inward journey. There is more to us than we know and to put all the emphasis on the concrete problem can blind us to the underlying dynamics and the possibility of doing something more constructive about ourselves and our personal difficulties.

The point to remember is that *we need not rid ourselves of troublesome behavior immediately.* Whatever it is—phobias, obsessions, or depression—we can live with it awhile if we are intelligently and compassionately trying to understand it in terms of our overall personality. If we don't feel compelled to resolve that we will never do this or that again we will avoid a great deal of frustration. After all, we are almost sure to repeat something that has deep roots in us whether we want to or not. A more patient effort to understand, and perhaps to get some additional help, relieves our tension and is far more constructive. If we do not try to rid ourselves of the troublesome behavior, neither should we indulge the behavior as though it were an indifferent matter. It is dangerous to rationalize strange behavior, although this is a frequent practice on the part of people who are unwilling to look beneath the surface in order to trace down its origins more carefully. That kind of rationalization does not serve us very well or for very long. A proper respect for ourselves dictates a compassionate effort always to see ourselves whole. We can do something about our troubles but it only lasts if it is the outcome of insight rather than impulsive and all-embracing resolutions.

End Products

Troubles surface in symptoms, the indirect signals of conflict and of our effort to handle it without coming fully to grips with it. The external symptoms on the surface can be bewildering until we begin to read them as a special language. Basic to our understanding is an appreciation that these symptoms—much like the symptoms in physical illness—are actually the evidence of the personality's effort to solve a more basic conflict. The symptoms are not the problem in themselves. They are to our internal conflict as fever is to the infection, efforts at regulating the processes more than problems to be solved in and of themselves.

It is also helpful to recall that *the things that drive us crazy about people are generally the things that are keeping them sane.* The outer problems, things that annoy us about them, are frequently their symptom manifestations, the psychological processes by which they manage the pressures on their inner personalities. They cannot exist without these symptomatic difficulties; they enable them to get by without giving in completely to a total collapse. And so it operates for ourselves. Our problems may annoy us very much but they are functional; they enable us to get by until we can get at the heart of the problem. They keep us together, not in ideal fashion, but together nonetheless. They should not be isolated from the total context of our reacting personality.

There are symptoms for every kind of psychological difficulty but we will confine ourselves to a few that are common among relatively healthy individuals. There are symptoms, for example, that are characteristic of the whole range of *adjustment reactions.* Adjustment reactions are not examples of neurotic behavior. They are rather typical of the problems that healthy people have all the time, especially when they are subjected to great stress or to some serious loss, as of a loved one, in their life. Everybody reacts to these things. And much of the behavior we see at these times is symbolic and only poorly understood even by the most sophisticated of scientists. Adjustment reactions usually include the experience of anxiety and the family of behaviors associated with this. They also give rise to psychophysiologic disturbances, the more recent term for psychosomatic disorders. This merely indicates that persons react in a total fashion to life rather than in any one aspect of their personalities. There are also behavioral disturbances. People under stress or in the wake of a loss, as during a period of grief or mourning, do unusual things which they have never done before. We should not think that this means that the world is ending. This symbolic dealing with the difficulty usually goes away, as do these other signs, when the stress is removed or when the loss has been handled psychologically. Other reactions that take place when we are trying to adjust to a major shift in the circumstances of our lives include a lowering of efficiency and a decrease in our morale. We should expect these occurrences at difficult points in our lives.

Neurotic Reactions

Neurotic reactions are quite varied. They spring ordinarily from internal conflicts that take place on the unconscious level. The kind of defenses a person uses in dealing with this conflict produces a special—and typical—look to the emerging neurosis. The external neurotic style tells us something about the underlying conflict and also something about the general personality patterns of the individuals suffering it. Our problems fit us; they match what we are like. Our symptoms, in other words, are instructive about who we are; they flow from our personal emotional foundations. Our symptoms may look odd but they allow us to manage our way through life without getting any worse. They keep our anxiety manageable. Neurotic reactions will be discussed in greater detail later on. For now it is helpful to realize that they generally affect only one aspect of the personality. The rest of the individual may well remain pleasingly normal. A neurosis is a mild disability marked by such things as obsessions, compulsions, and phobias. The affected person keeps in touch with reality, however, while experiencing the painful and disruptive neurosis. We handle our troubles much more easily when we have an appreciation of their nature. Taking what we can of the unknown away from them is a great help to us.

3

Nobody Has It All Together

The first principle in being human toward ourselves is based on the universal and exceptionless truth that nobody has it all together. It only looks that way.

And it only looks that way to us because we are glancing at other people from our own angle. We see them from the outside and we compare them to ourselves and judge that they have outwitted life, found the secret of youth, or lead totally untroubled existences. They seem to have everything that we ourselves want or think that we need. The hitch is that we can only see them from our angle and that we impose our own standards on them in the process. We also tend to judge ourselves more harshly, give ourselves fewer breaks, and generally less credit for our accomplishments. We cannot see the inner world of struggle and trouble that besets persons who seem so poised and confident to us. They are almost maddeningly at peace with the world as far as we are concerned. We are intimidated by what appears to be not only their success but the fact that they seem to be enjoying it so much.

The truth is, of course, that nobody does have it all together and most people don't feel that they do although they think everybody else does. They feel like something is missing and they spend a lot of time and effort in trying to discover what it is. When they look over the fence at somebody else's yard, however, their uneasiness only increases. Such comparisons not only make us despise our lot more but they frequently spur us to imprudent courses of action; envy and jealousy move us to do things that, in the long run, do us more harm than good. When we are caught up in a world in which we think that everybody else is doing better than we are our lives get more rather than less complicated. Some may be doing better, others worse, but most of us are muddling along trying to keep a balance between our assets and our liabilities, hoping to get through the day or the week without the walls of our existence collapsing on us.

There is a steady tension involved in purposeful living. Nobody ever beats life completely or arrives at a point where they have nothing to worry about and nothing to strive for. Should a person get into that situation the only thing left remaining on the agenda might be to die. That is probably exactly what some individuals do when they have run out of goals and don't know where to look to find aims or experiences that would deliver added meaning to their lives. The game of comparing ourselves to others in itself is a major trouble. We are all burdened and, no matter how great a person's achievement, its meaning is in the active achievement rather than in the final accomplishment. Getting this done or getting that done, surmounting this difficulty or solving that problem: These are worthy and humanizing experiences when they are approached with integrity but, like all things, they come to an end and we must find something else to take up our attention. We cannot go through life like bores at a party who want to tell us about the swimming medals they won in high school. There is a progressive dynamic involved in life, in other words, that means it is essentially impossible ever to get it all together. We keep at it and when we do this with purpose and a fairly well-developed sense of ourselves, we are at peace and we are happy. But we are not without troubles.

It is not in the nature of things for human beings to be able to reach any point at which they can finally say, "I have done it." There are, indeed, challenges that keep coming to human beings all through the life cycle. Some of them cannot be appreciated, much less undertaken, until we have reached the age in which they can make some sense to us. There are tasks, as we all know, that we can only take up in old age, after we have retired or finished the main body of our active work or career. Retirement does not mean somnolence in Sun City. There is always important human work to do and it concerns our sense of ourselves, our relationship to our families and our concern for mankind and for the generations that come after us. Challenges pile up as we must progressively deal with the loss of friends and close members of our families, profound challenges not to give up but to let go of things that we have held close for many years. Nobody can do that until they arrive at the age when these become the tasks that predominate. Each life stage has its special tasks, and we meet them only as we mature. They wait for us. We never get over life, in other words, and there is forever something fresh, some new challenge to our creativity no matter how old we get. Coming to terms with death is the final challenge for each of us.

We do not have to think of great things, not even the sharply defining events of any stage of our life, to understand the limitations on getting life under our thumb at any time. Frustration is built into existence; we cannot close our hands on its deepest experiences and our failure only deepens our longing. Anticipation plays a great role in life, far greater in most activities, as has been mentioned before, than the actual realization of the accomplishment. This goes for things as far different as writing a book and taking a vacation. The interesting part about writing a book is writing it. It is also the stressful part but authors know that as they turn to the typewriter every day and engage their powers once more in the struggle to get experience into words they are doing that which they enjoy most. There is a tension associated with getting a book written that, for them, is like no other experience. It is far more satisfying than is the finishing of a book. It is not uncommon for authors to lose interest in books once they are finished and sent to the printers. Paralleled in many other experiences, this underscores the nature of engagement, of striving toward a goal—of an essentially dynamic commitment of the self—which is close to the center of contented living. Having it done is nothing like doing it. Most of the surveys that try to uncover the happiest portions of people's lives isolate the moments of struggle and of uncertainty, the times of building and setting out in life, as the richest. Getting it all together beats having it all together.

But these experiences cannot be frozen. They are of their very nature shifting and mercurial. They are existentially powerful and almost impossible to measure. One must reflect on this to develop a constructive mode of handling life's problems. It is not cynical to ask, for example, how often anybody ever gets what they really want in life. They may get something close to it or they may get all of it for a while but nobody gets all of it all the time. Even in an ordinary day's activities how often do we get to do the thing we really choose to do most enthusiastically if everything else could be gotten out of the way. Would it be to read a book for a few uninterrupted moments, do some sewing or other work we would enjoy, just watch the birds as they migrate, or go to a play, or even take a walk? Each one of these activities, simple but profound, is circumscribed by time and events, by things that come before and by things that follow after. They are worth looking forward to and then they slip by almost before we can focus on them enough to enjoy them. Part of the way to deal with the troubles of life is to try to get the present into sharper focus, to get the most out of life by entering fully into such experiences rather than treating them like dull agenda items. It takes a feeling for time to make these moments more fully ours.

But there are limitations even to entering into our experience that give us hints of mystery and a sense of what the eternal is like. They allow us to feel the longing edge of our own unconscious selves. This happens when we get to do what we want or to go where we want and suddenly begin to realize that the anticipation is over. We are already spending the capital of our free time, our vacation, or our communion with someone we love deeply. It can happen in almost any activity we define as human. We may aspire to a career and, through long struggle and education, attain it and then discover that we have all the liabilities that go with it as well. We become a famous surgeon but the malpractice rates are dizzying. We are finally admitted to the bar only to have the ethical sense and prestige of the profession brought under question. We are elected to office only to find that people trust garbage collectors more than us. We enter the service of the Church only to find the security that once characterized that profession as practically nonexistent. Everywhere we go we run into the loose ends of things. We find that living deeply has side effects for which we may not be prepared or which may disappoint or disillusion us. There is almost always a fly—or signs that the fly has been there—in the ointment.

What are we to do, despair? No, we may rejoice because we have begun to understand that the trouble with living is our chief trouble. It is a good kind of trouble, this jagged crack across our experience. It is compounded of the penalty of time, our own imperfection and our own longing for something deeper and more lasting. It is always there and, when we realize it, we can take life a little more in stride. We will be less rushed and less panicked, less pressed to try to get it all together when just keeping it pretty well together is a major accomplishment in itself.

This does not mean that we should settle for being immature. It suggests that the beginning of wisdom is to understand that it is in running the race and involving ourselves in life that we enjoy all the best parts of it. But we also come up against inevitable difficulties at the same time. We will never have it all together but there is nothing wrong with that. Unfortunately, modern culture has a way of rewarding immaturity, prompting it as supposedly desirable behavior on the part of its citizens, of offering less than half a loaf and denying people a vision of what they must understand in order to appreciate and live their own lives in more satisfying fashion. We cannot conquer the world or have only happy endings or sunny days; we will never be trouble-free. This is a basic and constant truth which, if we can make it our own, saves us from an enormous amount of unnecessary trouble in life. There are some things we can understand about getting it together in life, however, and these include some of the following notions:

We never get it all together by ourselves. Life is a social process even though we may put ourselves first in our affections or our attentions, even though we may blot others out successfully for a while. What goes into getting life together—what produces the kinds of satisfactions that enable us to understand and deal with life purposefully—depends on the quality of our relationships with other persons. We do not possess all the resources by ourselves. In fact, we cannot even discover or be aware of them without the presence of other persons in our lives. We must let them in even though they are a source of a great deal of trouble. There will be many days on which people will repeat the old phrase that "people are no damn good," but there is no living that means anything without them. People mean trouble but they also mean life. The style we have in dealing with them tells us a lot about our possibility of ever getting what is important together. If we try only to dominate other persons, if we are only afraid of them and so try to avoid them, we make our chances of sensing the unity of our lives more remote.

Our lives look pretty much the way we want them. Even our troubles are the kind that we choose. It suits us to have these, especially if we have had them for a long while, and even when they seem a great puzzle to us. This is a signal that we are meeting some personal need, even if it is only at an unconscious level of existence. Our lives, however, are not fashioned by fate and if they seem to be undone and far from all together, it may well be because we need to have them that way. We keep getting ourselves into certain situations because we need the stimulation, the incidental excitement, or the resulting punishment in order to keep going. We may profit from asking ourselves what we are getting out of what seem to be the great difficulties that are regularly a part of our lives. They are not there accidentally. We have something to do with them. We are the designers at some level of our own existence.

Life is lived, for the most part, in very ordinary ways. We need to be reminded of the unspectacular quality of most of our existence. We have to think again about the fact that those experiences which are most meaningful to us are in themselves quite common. These include an adequate sense of ourselves, the kind of self-esteem that comes from realizing our abilities through living our own truths and possibilities. Vital to our understanding of what it means to be a human being is the capacity to share friendship and love with other persons. Closely related to this is our ability to do work that expresses what is true about ourselves while it also adds to general wealth of life around us. Life has a lot to do with such simple but profound things. The terrible fate of many persons whose lives seem troubled now is that they never recognized that the mystery of life springs from these events and occasions, that the great celebration of existence is not in adventurous enterprise or achievement but in being able to enter deeply into these commonplace experiences. Many people have been sold a bill of goods, in other words, and have been offered goals in a consumer society which have been cruelly deceptive. They have felt that if they could fulfill the desires they have been manipulated into having they would have a sense of completion about themselves. But consuming things that are not really essential to the experience of being human is just a way of failing to be human enough to ourselves. Frills on the surface of things, even great trips or powerful cars—the things that have been sold as dreams to people in abundance—have left them feeling at least half empty. They try for the things they don't need and they end up lacking the things that they need desperately. They think they have it all together because they have managed to get the right clothes, sing the right music, or be at the right places. But they are like corpses at a fancy mortuary. They look wonderful but they are not going anywhere.

There are many important things that we never get together. It is in pursuing them or deepening our appreciation of them that we lay hold of life itself. These are things that we simply never master or say the last words about. They include loving somebody truly and being loved in return. Number here as well the countless adventures that go into raising a family or teaching a class of students or working together with people toward a worthwhile goal. Count also being a friend in time of need or not. There is no way we ever get that all together. We just go on being a friend and it always requires something new from us. None of the best experiences of life depend on an old repertoire of responses. They are satisfying precisely because they always ask something new of us and of our personalities. They ask us to keep getting it together.

Understanding ourselves is something we never get all together. The unconscious reservoir is just too deep. We continue to be capable of surprising ourselves. There is something dreadfully dull about people who have analyzed themselves to death. The worst loss they suffer is that they can no longer surprise themselves, that they can no longer discover something they did not know was there. They seem dry and a little dusty; they have lost a major part of their capacity for enjoying life.

There are other experiences, like *praying,* for example, that we never really get all together either. People spend a great deal of energy trying to get these things done, trying to hone them to a certain perfection. But we never do and this is a source of great disappointment for some people. They find that they can still make beginner's mistakes, that what they thought they had finally conquered has risen once more to conquer them. Some rich experiences consist always in starting fresh on them.

The vital signs we find in the lives of people are very simple ones. There is a certain peace and contentment experienced by persons who know that the imperfect pursuit of an always better performance is a very high achievement. There is great validity in the lives of persons who are honest enough to face their faults, to make room for them, and not to despise themselves or others because of the liabilities attached to existence. Joy is what we can identify in the lives of people who are not afraid of life and who meet it very much on its own terms. They know that the challenge never ends and that the troubles are never completely overcome. Such persons are well equipped to deal constructively with the numberless troubles of life itself; that, in fact, is how they spend their lives.

Bad Signs

There are things to watch for, evidence that suggests that we should take some positive steps to shake ourselves loose from the adjustment in which we are caught. These include some of the following:

Treating ourselves as objects. This is the opposite of regarding ourselves as subjects in life. When we are subjects we can voice an *I* that speaks clearly for our total identity. As subjects we inhabit our true personality. We are aware of the wide range of feelings and other internal behaviors that define us. We make our own decisions, however, and we even make our own mistakes. As subjects in life we respect ourselves. Being an object, even in our own eyes, means that we look at ourselves from a detached point of view. We do not feel our own wholeness; we do not experience ourselves in terms of our unique identity. We are always standing at a distance; we are outside looking in. We may, for example, treat ourselves as an object by going through life trying to find out how to please other persons all the time. That means that we never respond to our own best instincts, trust our own judgment, or feel deep operational respect for ourselves. In these circumstances we need the approval of someone else to feel that we are worthwhile.

We treat ourselves as objects *when we think about ourselves in the third person.* Again, this is a distancing maneuver. We regard ourselves from afar, observing ourselves and living largely by rules or aphorisms from outside of us. An individual lives in the third person, for example, when, in response, to a challenge in life, he or she makes a decision by saying something like this: "A good husband would do this . . ."; "A good mother does this . . ."; "A good teacher does this . . ." That is living off somebody else's capital. It keeps us from the exhilaration of a subjective taste of life.

If You Had Your Life to Live Over

People talk about this a lot. They do not do it seriously most of the time but occasionally they do wonder about what would have happened if they had taken that other fork in the road, made a different decision, or met somebody else at a specific time in their lives. It may be worth thinking about. What would you do if you had your life to live over. What do you think you could do about it?

This can be made practical if we devise a kind of test in which we take incomplete sentences and finish them with what spontaneously comes to our minds. For example, take the sentence "My biggest error . . ." How would we finish this? Or, "One thing I would like to change . . ." "I would be happy if . . ." These sentences are not meant to increase regrets but to stimulate thinking in a realistic manner about what and whether we would change very much about ourselves. These sentences spur us to reexamine ourselves in terms of our own life situation. Be fair and be honest, as fair with yourself as you would be with somebody else. You may just find that you have not done just half bad after all. You will certainly be less hard on yourself—and less envious of others—in judging what having it all together means.

4

What It Means to Be Yourself

Everybody wants to sing the same songs these days: "I gotta be me" or "I did it my way." Unfortunately, these songs represent more wish than reality, more an elusive ideal rather than a firm achievement. Most persons like to think that, above all else, they are, as another popular saying goes, "their own person." But very few people who boast about it a lot are really that way. Being truly one's self does not mean being rich, powerful, or indifferent enough to the feelings of others to be able to do whatever we want. It doesn't mean private islands and private jets and public envy of one's position. It is far simpler, as most good things in life are, and far more wrenching of the spirit because being one's self, paradoxically enough, is built on putting an end to selfishness.

The notion of being one's self has come popularly to signify living as though there were no world around us, as though we could strike away the limits the way we might strike chains off a prisoner. This romantic notion of being an individual suggests that no considerations of reality need impinge on our private worlds. It would be a strange world indeed because there would be no people in it who would make much of a difference to us, not difference enough for us to sacrifice any of our own aims or desires for their sake. Being oneself in this popular sense is a return to childhood, to a happy world in which we are indeed the center and where others exist to meet our needs.

Being oneself, in this sense, means ridding oneself of the necessary trouble of being in relationship to other persons all the time. Like all corruptions, of course, there is some truth in the middle of the gritty selfishness that goes into trying to reconstruct the childhood world. "Doing it my way" too often means a somewhat blind insistence on one's own will in a world that must nourish us whenever we demand it. Now there's an attitude that can cause trouble.

Being oneself has also been closely identified with the notion of being eccentric, standing out as markedly different from other persons. Indeed, the streets are filled with bizarre-looking characters all the time. Such characters don't look quite so different anymore. In the heady search for contemporary individuality everybody is beginning to look bizarre. They hurry to present themselves as rebels against society, feeling good that their dress or their behavior in some way seems to challenge that wonderful anonymous enemy, the establishment. It's good to recall that psychopaths also delight in making their own rules and that mass bizarreness, or stylish eccentricity, makes people less rather than more individualistic.

Is being at odds with society necessarily the key to individuality? There are other explanations to eccentric behavior and we should attend to some of these before we commit ourselves in person or in principle to ways of acting that are neither adult nor individual. It is possible, for example, that some people who indulge in eccentric behavior or determined individuality are actually trying to finish their adolescent growth in public. People do, of course, want to finish their growing and in our day and age they often end up doing it in front of everybody else. There is a certain freedom to indulge their desires by dressing, for example, like a cowboy when they are actually a copywriter, or to wear expensive, artificially aged workingmen's clothes in executive suites. The poor would not dress that way if they could make a choice; it is only a luxury that can be afforded by the affluent. This is not a terribly serious social problem. These people generally do look adolescent anyway. Do they think they are fooling us? It is perfectly all right for persons to act out a little, to indulge a minor exhibitionistic need, or to try to get attention by means which, if anything, constitute a very mild protest against the general rules of society. Society encourages and subsidizes such carrying on; it is good for business. There is no great harm in it but there is hardly any individuality either. The best testimony to this is found in the indistinguishable hordes of people who have chosen to protest against conventionality in exactly the same way. Sooner or later these people will escape adolescence, perhaps as it collapses like a burning shack around them, or when, at some future date, they discover that their high style has failed to make them either individual or mature.

Being oneself does not mean being conventionally bizarre. And there is a great deal of unhappy conformity going on in a wide range of matters. It includes living off the opinions of others on most major subjects. It is startling, for example, to note how many self-styled individuals uncritically accept the convention or romantic wisdom of the day on subjects like sex and marriage. It is an indulgence that delivers a mild thrill and the secret joy of being somewhat wicked. It is not, however, adulthood. It is more trouble, really, than being a genuine individual.

More serious is the dependence of this kind of conformity on surfaces, on the appearance rather than on the substance of things. This is reflected, perhaps better than anywhere else, in contemporary movies where so much is made of getting the right look and the right feel of things. You think you are in Chicago in 1936 or in Los Angeles in 1968, the latter date significant in the film *Shampoo* which has had such a good track record at box offices throughout the world. The picture is exactly right for the surfaces of the people and the events of election day 1968; it is, however, all surface and it stumbles badly because it cannot represent the inner motivations of the characters involved. It fails artistically because it is such a human failure. Everybody in it is stylishly empty. Yet it may reflect the preoccupation of a country that seems to seek individuality through a manipulation of surface qualities far more than through a realization of inner character.

This is not to condemn any of these manifestations of America trying to work out its adolescence in public. There is plenty of other evidence to support it from the flood of *Playboy*-like magazines which still indulge the male-chauvinist life-style and whose philosophy is too feeble to take or to criticize seriously. It has little relationship to living in depth and very little feel of what it means to take on the trouble of developing oneself as an individual person.

Being yourself is actually the work of a lifetime. We can indulge such aberrations as pretending to be rebels by wearing workingmen's clothes. These are just footnotes to the continuing trouble that is involved in achieving adulthood. We need some of these indulgences to support ourselves, to bolster our egos in a superficial way, but for short periods of time. It is like going to a party in which we suspend the ordinary business of life and allow ourselves to break at least some rules of ordinary behavior. It fits the nature of human beings to do such things. We don't bolster our individuality by becoming fiercely somber Puritans who give no leeway to the human need for fun.

Becoming an adult individual is a large part of the unfinished business that we keep working on all the time. We never get it down perfectly. We are always finding out new and surprising things about ourselves, having ourselves challenged when we do not expect it, or finding that no matter how often we may prove ourselves there is always a new test for us just around the corner.

Becoming ourselves may well depend on being able to sort out what is adolescent from what is adult in us. It makes sense to make that distinction. We can always discover signs of continuing adolescence in us and, as long as we can name them correctly, we will not be tempted to hold them up to the world as proof that we have arrived at maturity. We may have to learn to live with these signs for a while. There is nothing wrong with that because we cannot dismiss them overnight. We may all have a little in us of the Teddy Roosevelt who, having completed his terms in the White House, contemplated a trip to Africa with the phrase "It's my last chance to be a boy again." But recognizing our urge and our willingness at times to be adolescent in order to soften the harsh demands of reality is far different from mistaking that for a high level of individual growth.

A person who in mid-life contemplates a major career change is not necessarily indulging in an adolescent fantasy. This may be a sign that the individual has put adolescence behind, has solidified his or her sense of values, and is prepared to take a truly existential risk in giving up security to achieve a new ideal. The elements of maturity will be obvious, however, because the decision will not be impulsive, ill-thought-out, nor will it unnecessarily subject other persons to unusual hardship or deprivation. The elements involved will be weighed carefully and serious soul-searching that reveals that the person can get beneath the surface of life will also be obvious. In short, it will not have the marks of a whim but of a serious decision. A lot of people in middle age do funny things in order to finish their adolescence. They do them precipitously and frequently with little regard to the damage done to others in the process. Families are broken up, marriages are ended, and new careers are undertaken without deeply serious reflection. One feels that some of these things happen because it is in the air, that giving up one's contracted responsibilities and commitments in order to find a new and independent life has suddenly become more than acceptable. It is highly questionable, however, that decisions that take away the life of spouse or children to any degree can really, in the long run, promote life in the one who makes them.

Persons interested in individuality do not listen only in the first place to what the noisy world tells them. Such persons listen carefully and respectfully to themselves. They are aware of the complexity of their personalities and they do not mistreat them, moving impulsively in response to what amounts to a passing fad rather than a genuine conviction. They take themselves seriously enough to treat themselves respectfully.

Listening this way involves us in an arduous and continuing activity. If, however, we can hear what our feelings tell us we will be well informed about ourselves and the choices we make in life. We will emerge more clearly as individuals if we can interpret the signals that come from our feelings accurately. But this is not easy business and it is not to be confused with an automatic response to impulse. Listening to ourselves, as we have observed, implies a readiness to trace our feelings to their source and to try to distinguish between the many motivations that may lead us to action. A person, for example, may feel like confronting his boss on a certain issue. He may report that he wishes to do this because he feels that in conscience some principle has been violated and that he must speak up about it. It is also possible, however, if he analyzes his emotions, that complications could be present. If he listens carefully he may discover that his paranoid boss has tripped off in him a reaction that is not adult but is rather an irrational and uncharacteristic need to prove that he is a man. Crazy people get us to do crazy things in trying to prove that we are sane. Such a decision, in other words, may play right into the boss's hands, just as we play into the hands of children when we respond with anger—but also with the attention they want—to their aggravations. People know how to get us to do things we would not ordinarily do and the person who is an adult individual is capable of distinguishing between these two behaviors. We can understand the urge but also pinpoint its origin and make a decision not to act upon it. Hundreds of examples like this could be given to cover a wide range of feelings from the irritable to the erotic. It takes a real individual to hear what is going on and to make sense of the messages, not all of which demand that we act on them in order to prove that we are being ourselves.

Another aspect of this which is quite important concerns our individual ethnic, cultural, and religious traditions. These are part of us in more than a poetic way. Something of our soul has been shaped by the experience of our ancestors and by the environments in which we have grown up. We must respect rather than reject these inheritances out of hand. It had been very much in style, however, to look away from our beginnings until the recent ethnic consciousness began to assert itself in the land. Psychologically speaking, our origins are essential for achieving our individuality. All one needs to do is to inspect the lives of people who have cut off their own cultural or religious roots. They have suffered a loss in a crucial aspect of their identity and they frequently exhibit personalities that seem to have holes in them. They may be very modern in being estranged from the rituals of their tradition but they are also very empty. They are forever searching for the lost base on which to stand as individuals.

Traditions and rituals are a special language of the unconscious. As we have observed earlier, the unconscious is a significant part of our personalities, and to deny it the kind of expression it gets in the symbolic behavior that transcends the rational is to mistreat ourselves. We commit sacrilege when we cut ourselves off from the rites and rituals which speak to and express our depths in a highly important way. We fail thereby to nourish the unconscious and, therefore, to nourish our own individuality. This absence of symbolic dialogue is a distinguishing characteristic of many contemporary individuals. It leaves a peculiarly modern ache that is difficult to diagnose. It has to do, however, with their identity and with the aspects of themselves which are real and which, if ignored, cause a spiritual pain that is not responded to by affluence, stylish infidelities, or any of the other aspects of acted-out adolescence which can be observed so widely today.

It is also essential for people who want to be themselves to recognize the social nature of human development. We never find our true selves alone nor can we isolate our growth from that of other persons. As adults we forge our full development in the crucible that is called intimacy. We cannot go it alone and feel that such hardihood is a sign of our individuality. Maturity must master the lessons of reciprocity. We become adults in the context of taking account of and responding to what is true and significant in those persons who live close to us. This state of activity cannot be cut off as though it were a matter of indifference. We must learn what it means to experience a healthy dependency on another person. We must give ourselves over to the experiences that require sacrifice and patience and an ever more finely honed sensitivity to the rights and feelings of other individuals. We become individuals in relationship, not in isolation.

Being oneself in many contemporary scenarios means abandoning all of this. It pulls oneself on center stage, the ego unbound seeking its satisfactions at the expense of rather than in relationship to others. The true attainment of individuality is impossible, however, without a practical and loving way of living with other persons. Perhaps the most important characteristic of adulthood is the capacity to take the presence of others in our lives into account. We are adult individuals when we realize that we cannot have life all our own way, that we cannot live on the energy of impulse, and that we will always be working out our individuality in the creative tension of relationships with other persons. We become ourselves when we give up the unnecessary trouble that goes with hiding ourselves from others.

If we are going to be adults we will always be in trouble. The trouble is that we live in a world where the dream of individuality can be a childish reverie if we do not see our fate as intimately bound up with the way we live and grow with other persons. Love is the name we give to that and it is a lot of trouble. It is the chief trouble but, to those who experience it, it is obviously the most necessary of all our troubles.

Principles of Individuation

In pursuing our own identity it is helpful to remember that the more we try to act like adults the more we usually look like adolescents. The more we strive to assume adult ways when these are not truly expressive of our level of growth, the more obvious it will be to other persons that we are pretending rather than acting spontaneously. One can observe and understand this in adolescents as they self-consciously strive, perhaps on their first night in evening clothes, to act in super-suave ways. It is all right for them to betray the fact that they are still adolescents. It is clear, in fact, that the more they try to act like they are forty years old the more obvious it is that they are still seventeen. It is understandable then, there is so much trouble connected with growing up. But such behavior is a danger signal for adults. The more we insist that we are going to do things "my way" the more we reveal just how much growing up lies still before us.

Old Laws that are Always New

There are staples to living maturely that have never been improved upon. Remembering only a few of them will help us handle the troubles of life far more surely.

We have to delay most gratifications in life. This is practically heresy in the contemporary world but it remains true. Nevertheless, we cannot grab at what we want and take it at any time. There is a great measure of waiting involved in anything that is worthwhile in life. One of the best indicators of adulthood remains our ability to postpone getting what we want because we acknowledge the rights and concerns of other persons. The less we insist on our sole rights the more individual we become. Only a child grasps at gratifications without any sense of this. Impulsive egotism is not the same as being "one's own person."

We can't have it all. A wise person saves a lot of trouble by living with respect for this reality rather than by some vain and sure-to-be-frustrated effort to lay claim to everything. There is a simple wisdom in understanding that, no matter what we are talking about, there is no way in which we can have everything we want. We have to make certain settlements, certain give-and-take compromises, in order to live adult individual lives. That is not the same as cynicism or abandoning the efforts to develop ourselves. It means that we live in a real world, with a real life history and inheritance, and that, if we are to survive psychologically, we live in the company of other persons. It means that we accept the limitations of the human condition and enter into rather than attempt to deny it.

We are mature individuals not when we know what we want and how to get it but when we understand what we possess of value and know how to give it away freely. The paradox of the truth involved in individuality is that it rests not on taking but on giving. That depends on our having some resources to share with others and a loving willingness to do just that. There is more giving by far than taking involved in a mature life. It seems like a lot of trouble; it is the trouble that makes life take on meaning. It is the thing we do when we understand something about the nature of mature love. Giving is the key to all our success as individuals and in our relationships. Nothing has turned out to be an improvement on it. Being willing to die to ourselves is the trouble of troubles but it is still the way to a fuller life.

5

The Common Cold of Troubles

The absence of troubles, like the discovery of the Fountain of Youth, remains an alluring but impossible dream. We never get rid of troubles although we can get better at dealing with them. We can even learn to lessen their impact and sometimes turn them to our advantage. Just to lessen their impact, however, is no small goal, especially in a world where there is always harvest of necessary troubles to attract our attention and to test our capacity to adjust to them.

Adjustment difficulties, as mentioned before, is the general term used by psychology to describe that array of problems that are intimately associated with ordinary living. They generally occur serially but they can also come in clusters. There are very few periods in life in which we are free of them. These breathing spaces are great blessings but they are not permanent states. There is little time left between the occurrence of the stresses that challenge our ability to adjust and to readjust constantly to life.

Take a house, for example, as a complex, almost living, set of problems known well to all mortgaged homeowners. There seems to be an internal timing system in a house, somewhat like the time-released ingredients in certain capsuled medicines, that manages to keep stress at a fairly intense level. One year the furnace starts acting up. A month after that it is expensively repaired. The price of oil and coal rises. A month after that, just as the homeowners are settling back, strange knockings sound in the plumbing. Clear that up and the roof that seemed so durable suddenly begins to disintegrate. All of these problems can be handled, of course, but each one introduces a new measure of stress into life. When they come in clusters the stresses multiply and the effect can be quite damaging.

Such occurrences fill the average life, generating stress that is like a hard blowing wind making us squint and hunch ourselves together in order to continue on our journey. Examples of these common pressure-filled situations which demand adjustments on our part include the death of a loved one, separation from family or friends, the loss of a job, the experience of divorce, a major illness, moving or transferring jobs, getting married, or retiring. There is a certain amount of stress associated with creative activities, such as negotiating a successful business deal or even writing a poem; but this side-effect kind of stress is part of an experience that is intrinsically enhancing to the overall person. The components of the destructive stress that eats away at personality and demands adjustment include, first of all, a difficult situation faced by an individual whose functioning is within normal psychological limits. The key to the stress generated is that the way in which the individual ordinarily handles this stress of life no longer works well. Something breaks down in the way the person copes with this particular problem. This failure in psychological adjustment generates a varied set of symptoms that are typical of these reactions. The adjustment reaction, then, is common and may be observed in those life experiences that cause insecurity and take away our ordinary satisfactions, and, in the face of these, we find that our usual responses no longer work.

What are some of the symptoms that occur in connection with this pervasive adjustment reaction? Anxiety appears in various forms. Persons experiencing stress that they cannot handle in their usual way find that they are excessively worried, "on edge," as they say, that they cannot get to sleep or they wake early in the morning; they cannot enjoy their food or do not eat regularly or properly. There may also be a harvest of symbolic problems manifested in psychophysiologic disorders. These include the well-recognized disturbances of the gastro-intestinal tract that so many persons experience when they are having difficulties in managing stress. Persons also find that they are less efficient than they ordinarily are. They are easily distracted and somewhat depressed. They cannot seem to concentrate on their work as they ordinarily do. They are, as they unconsciously but accurately describe themselves, "out of it" or "beside themselves."

Because our ordinary way of dealing with this problem no longer works well we may try other solutions which, in the long run—and sometimes in the short run—don't work very well either. A typical example of what is described as a "maladaptive" solution—something we would ordinarily never do—is when we get mad because we are frustrated in love or at work. Getting mad through becoming assaultive or abrasive has never helped a manager to get the umpire to change a decision in a baseball game and is no more effective in helping human beings faced with a major life trouble. It is an effort at solution that is obviously ineffective and alienating. Closely related are the efforts individuals sometimes make to reduce their experience of anxiety. Here too they do things which are not really effective and which may further damage their sense of themselves in their relationships with others. Drinking too much, for example, may lessen a person's concerns temporarily but it has never been known to take them away completely. Other strange behaviors in this regard include a sudden experience of promiscuity, gambling, staying away from work, or some other atypical strategy that is out of synchronization with the rest of their lives. Such behaviors must be understood as ill-suited efforts at solving some life problems. These are the things that normal people sometimes resort to under overwhelming stress when they cannot marshal their own forces in an effective way.

What can we do about this all-too-familiar problem? It is helpful for us to recognize the existence of these stresses and to admit the toll they take even of the strongest of human beings. Many Americans have inherited an ethic which makes them feel that they must bear everything without complaint, granting themselves little quarter if any at all, and in general not complain. This stoical way of handling existence presses a lid on conflicts, forcing them down into the unconscious, and leading to their symbolization in indirect ways. This is expressed by the leading character in Joseph Heller's novel *Something Happened.* Slocum, speaking of the stresses that he looks on as intrusions in his life says this: "I will not let myself cope with such human distress; I refuse to accept such realities; I dump it all right down into my unconscious and sit on it as hard as I can. Let it all come out in bad dreams if it has to. I forget them anyway as soon as I wake up."

Denying what affects us is imprudent and ineffective. The stresses of life show up whether we want to admit them or not. We cause ourselves a great deal of unnecessary trouble when we are unable to accept the fact that we are human enough to react like all other men and women in the face of difficult life circumstances. The ability to admit this as part of our picture of ourselves is an enormous help. We will not have any unrealistic expectations about holding everything in and insisting that nothing hurts when we are actually filled with inner anguish. Giving ourselves permission to feel life is a first step in being able to handle these common troubles more effectively.

It also helps to realize that most stresses that cause adjustment reactions are finite. They have a limited duration although the pressure can be very intense during that limited time. For example, a person preparing to take a major examination, such as that for admission to the bar, faces a definite period, of weeks or a few months at most, of intense preparation in which many of the ordinary activities of life will have to be suspended to prepare for and actually take the exam. There will be aftereffects for a while, as well. The person who anticipates this can make adequate preparation for this experience and will not be unduly alarmed or surprised at its effects. These will have been anticipated, much as the stock market has a way of sensing and discounting bad news in advance, so that the blow is not so bad during the actual event. The same principle applies for any other limited stress, such as making a difficult trip, appearing in a court trial, preparing a major talk, or even hosting a houseful of unpredictable guests for a weekend. Being able to perceive this as a limited experience which will take its toll is one way of making sure that we do not make this ordinary kind of trouble any worse.

Different are those situations which drag out without any clear sign of when they will terminate. The vagueness of these situations adds to the stress which they engender. To lose one's job during a recession, for example, and not to be sure when employment will be available again can become an enormous source of stress that is intensified because of the implications for the individual's self-esteem as a capable provider and an adult participating fully in life. Just the threat of job loss during the time of economic difficulty may be very stressful. People should not expect these experiences to be otherwise and, while the anticipation will not eliminate all the difficulties, it at least helps to be able to recognize that it is not unusual for us to react strongly when we are under a major stress situation. The longer the stress lasts the more the symptoms increase. It is possible that some of them will endure, much like scars after an operation, even after the stressful period has been terminated.

There are certain stresses that one can avoid, especially if one is already experiencing pressure from another life situation. It would not be sensible, for example, to invite the stress of a mother-in-law moving in at a time of marital misunderstanding and difficulties. Stress would only be multiplied foolishly if someone gambled life savings in a period of unemployment in some bizarre effort to recoup one's losses. We can avoid making our mistakes bigger than they already are, especially if we can check ourselves against reacting impulsively, that is, under the drive of high emotion during a period of stressful trouble. Unfortunately, emotions that are not understood can motivate us to decisions and actions that we perceive as solutions rather than as extended sources of stress. Such, for example, would be rushing into a marriage as though this in itself was a cure for one's problems. Marriage, in the judgment of most observers, adds to rather than diminishes the stress of human existence.

It does not help to worry outlandishly about things that have only a remote possibility of happening. When persons find that they are overly concerned about potential difficulties in life, when, for example, they ruminate obsessively about the possibilities of difficulties arising, they are borrowing troubles unnecessarily. This is usually the sign of some other kind of difficulty, an obsessive-compulsive problem, for example, and does not fall under the kind of anxiety that goes along with an adjustment difficulty in a stressful life situation.

It helps if, anticipating that life will have its stressful moments, we have a broad base on which to live in the first place. Reducing our world too narrowly, betting on too few people or too few interests, leaves us vulnerable in the extreme when these sources of satisfaction and security are under threat. Persons can have wide interests, can develop a sense of satisfaction from other activities besides their main occupation, and, above all, can deepen a sense of values about the meaning and purpose of life which will strengthen their capacity to sustain stressful situations. It is important for individuals to make use of the resources that are available in their own traditions, their religious views, and their general philosophy of life. Developing the spiritual side of personality—and this is something frequently ignored by advice givers who think that everything can be cured by smiling more or taking pills—is indispensable in becoming a mature adult. This is a very powerful source of support in stressful times.

It is basic to the effective handling of stressful situations to be able to talk about it with somebody else. We are not meant to go it alone through life. Stress is multiplied almost beyond endurance in the lives of people who think that they should not burden others with the problems that are bothering them. They tend to become impacted difficulties, and we are generally misguided or acting for some other reason than the one we suppose, when we are afraid that we will burden our friends or our loved ones by admitting to them that we are under stress. We burden them far more in the long run if the stress affects us negatively, alienates us from them, and leaves us, at least temporarily, psychologically upset. "If you had only told us about it," may be a sentence more full of regret than any other one in the English language. People are ready to listen if we give them a chance and let them know that something is important to us. We have to make an act of faith in them. That is precisely the kind of human activity that gains us support and additional inner strength to handle the stressful problems of life.

Practically speaking, individuals should not only anticipate the stressful troubles of life but should try to explore the concrete situation as thoroughly as possible once it has come upon them. This takes time and patience as well as an active capacity to listen to and control our own emotions.

Generally speaking, we have three possibilities when we are exposed to a stressful situation at home, at work, or in some other area of our lives. We can change the situation, leave the situation, or change ourselves in order to be able to cope more constructively with a situation that cannot be modified in itself. Sometimes, as in situations which seem to be traps where there is no good way out, we have to take the path that has the least liabilities connected with it. Often people discover that there are community resources available to assist them in periods of stress about which they had had no previous knowledge or which they stayed away from because they thought they only offered their services to the poor or to those who are out of work. There is a remarkable reservoir of willing people associated with community institutions that have been set up precisely to help people manage this stress better.

Perhaps the only sure thing we can do when we cannot do anything else about certain situations is to work on our own attitudes and our own perceptions of the difficulty. We can always do something about ourselves when we find it impossible to do anything about the world around us. This is an effective and sensible maneuver, one that depends on a willingness to look at ourselves and to try to understand what the possibilities of self-modification are in the situation. If we change ourselves—if, for example, we avoid bringing up combustible discussion topics with our live-in mother-in-law—we automatically change a whole environment. It becomes less stressful because we have eliminated one of the sources of stress by modifying our own conversational habits. This is an area in which our spiritual resources and our philosophy in life can be a great source of help to us. We can also inventory our interpersonal resources and make practical our belief in friends by broadening our base of relationship, deepening our sense of community with others, or by involving ourselves in worthwhile works of service during periods of strain and stress. There are a great number of such activities to attract our participation. Troubles lie ahead on everybody's horizon. The time to deal with them is before they happen. This allows us a period to anticipate various strategies and to prepare the personal resources needed to endure successfully these ever-recurring periods. Just as there is no cure for the common cold but only good ways to avoid it or to treat ourselves if we catch it, so there are many positive ways in which to prepare ourselves for the common cold of troubles, everyday stress.

6

The Trouble of Getting Along: An Inside Job

The way we get along with other persons defines and decides almost everything that is important about our lives. It tells the story of whether we are happy or sad, lonely or fulfilled, of whether we have understood what it means to be alive or have somehow missed the meaning of it along the way. Getting along with other persons—there is lots of trouble involved with this.

If this works well, life is a glowing success. The experience of intimacy is grown-up business, although it has been pursued in adolescent and sometimes childish ways in our culture. Because people have recognized the value of successful human relationships there has been an explosion of activity to discover the way to make getting along with each other work effectively in today's world. It is part of the American inheritance to try to solve problems or to achieve selected goals as swiftly and efficiently as possible. Intimacy has not yielded, however, to the psychological engineers who have promised it through a wide variety of treatments. Neither has it surrendered itself to those romantics who feel that if they could only be quit of life and its drudgery they would find the closeness of their dreams in some style of commune living. Americans have worked at love and friendship incessantly but many of them remain disappointed because they have not been able to get the results they long for. We have worked on marriage the way we have worked on the postal service in the United States and, trying to make them work, we have almost wrecked both of these institutions in the process.

But ordinary people want very simple things when you come right down to it. They do want their relationships to work. That is why they have tried so many of the remedies that have been offered to them in such profusion recently. They do not want to be lonely and they have an idea that if we find somebody else we can be close to we will also find life at the same time. That is a complicated business, however, and many people, seeking this experience, turn back disappointed, hurt, or just plain bewildered. The difficulty of getting along with others is large enough in itself. It is compounded, however, when we think about it only from the outside, from the viewpoint of devising a strategy through which to attack the difficulty.

Thinking about it from the outside goes along with all those efforts to solve life's problems that depend, for example, on being able to figure out other persons. We have the notion that if we can discover their secrets or understand their psychology we can gear ourselves better for a successful life with them. We can then devise the right combination of behavior or play on their needs and longings in order to draw them closer to us. It is well to remember, of course, that intimacy is not the same as sexuality. It is a far broader and richer term. Sexuality can be an important part of intimacy but it is only a part—and not always an essential part. You can be intimate without being sexual and you can certainly be sexual without being intimate. That is why many of the recipes for sexual success have been so disillusioning for people. They have tried to follow the instructions provided by the experts and, pleasurable though the mechanics of sexuality may be, they are not in and of themselves capable of delivering the deep and lasting kind of peaceful happiness that goes along with the successful experience of intimacy.

There is also a climate in the United States which provides

external services for a great many needs. It is not surprising that people should tend to externalize their problems. They do not look within themselves when they have a difficulty; they look rather around themselves to find the agency or the department designed by society to take care of this situation, whether it is for medical, psychological, or financial needs. This develops an attitude that notably handicaps people when they are challenged to look not outside but within themselves to understand their own emotions and the role they play in their life experiences.

Despite the explosion of interest in matters psychological, large numbers of people still do not think about themselves when they have problems getting along with others. They think of something that the other person can do, that an answer to prayer might provide, or that some external agency might supply. A small percentage of sensitive and insightful persons look first of all into their own human experience to understand what is happening when they encounter some difficulty in getting along with others in life. This kind of self-search is crucial, of course, to the informed life and to resolving the many-headed difficulties that rear up in the course of human relationships. This is not to say that everything that happens in our lives is our own fault any more than to say that everything that is right in our lives comes from our own individual enterprise or agency. We have to understand, that we, as parties of the first part, have a hand—some input at least—in causing what takes place in our lives. There is nothing accidental, nothing that springs from nowhere in human relationships. And there is very little that can be labeled as incidental. We are involved in some way in designing what happens to us. What we do, how we react, what things mean to us, all of these are significant if we are to analyze what occurs between ourselves and other persons. Taking the trouble to understand this takes care of a great many of our other troubles.

Not Just What We Say

Plenty goes on between us and even our most casual friends. It involves far more than our surface conversations. What we say is not nearly as important as how and why we say it. The words are the least of it all. Our exchanges with each other occur on many levels. The words that we use in speaking to each other should be important and accurate in reflecting what goes on between us. But this is only one aspect of the total experience that takes place between people who are friends.

The best question to ask if we want to pursue an understanding of the way we get along with people is very basic: *What does it mean to be in relationship to somebody?* It does not mean just to know them, nor just to have good times with them, nor to be able to use them or to be used by them in some way or other. One of the mysteries that makes life worthwhile centers on the significance of the rhythm and tone of our reciprocal ways in human relationships.

To be in relationship with another person means that we make some difference to them on a long-term basis. It also means that they make some difference to us, that when everything is added up and understood, we do not merely occupy adjacent space but that our lives and destinies are intermingled, that what we understand of ourselves is notably affected by how we stand in relationship to one another.

This is merely another way of describing how we are present to each other in life. It is easy to be next to others and not to be present to them. We can do it all the time, even if circumstances in which an observer might describe us as seeming to be very present to another person. Presence is a gift; we give it and we can only do this freely—just as we can withhold it. When we withhold our presence we change the nature of our relationship with others. It is the kind of thing that happens, for example, when friends have an argument. As a result they can temporarily withhold their presence from one another. This can be a very painful interlude. Such troubles would not happen if the persons did not make some difference to one another. Anybody who has experienced it can understand something of its existential force. It is akin to the loss we feel when a loved one must be separated from us. Absence of this kind helps us to understand what presence is all about.

Presence, therefore, although difficult to measure, is easy to understand. We can name those persons in whose lives we make a true and vibrant presence. In the same fashion, we can list those who make themselves present to us. There are many ways to water down psychological presence. These range from the decision to hold oneself back, as in the previous example, to the decay of presence that takes place when human beings do not work on their relationships with each other. Presence does not take care of itself. It is one of life's grandest blessings but, like everything else that significantly marks the mystery of human existence, it depends on our overall vitality and sense of ourselves, on our sensitivity and willingness to keep refining ourselves in relationship to others. It is as strong as we are and as weak as we can be when we let things go. Presence decays for many people who move slightly away from one another for whatever reason, and then begin to drift further and further away, thinking, at the edge of their minds perhaps, that they can always draw back close to one another again. It is frequently too late by the time they try to reverse their momentum. They have both changed. They can no longer provide the same kind of presence to each other.

The Trouble with Communication

Communication in friendship and marriage has been discussed endlessly and yet it remains a problem. Communication does not mean only external communication, although this has been featured in the advice that has suggested that the proper exchange of information, keeping each other abreast of what is going on, etc., is a help to friendship and marriage. There is no doubt that this information does help but information is not the soul of friendship and love. The communication of the spirit remains the essential ingredient and you cannot pin that on a kitchen bulletin board. You can tell people where you are every hour of the day and still remain quite elusive. This supplying of so much data merely frustrates people further. They seem to know everything and yet they seem to know nothing of each other. Such data may become a substitute for the essential communication of the inner person. Such sharing transcends facts and depends on open rather than categorized presence to each other. And on the amount of room they make for each other in their lives. Such communication is a question of the emotions more than of the intellect, of intuition rather than rational analysis. The heart has its reasons, the poet tells us, and sharing these, people break through to share something true and lasting of and with each other.

Communication is not a harsh or regressive activity, although it has become that in many of the movements and fads of the latter part of this century. To communicate with another person does not mean to assault them steadily with our inner anguish or problems. Communication is fundamentally a gentle activity. It does not mean to crash into somebody full force with all the ugly truths that we can convey; neither does it mean that we force the last ambiguous sentiment out of other persons. Friendship and love are not like therapy sessions.

The communication that characterizes friendship—and remains a clue for the understanding of ourselves that helps us to get along more successfully with others—depends on the analogy of being in communion with somebody else. This can be done without words, without gestures even, or without even touching each other at times. Without it, all the words, gestures, and touches mean very little. If, however, we can pool our psyches through an awareness of each other's lives and sensitivity to each other's needs, we automatically meet in an open place where communication is no longer a major or frustrating problem. The trouble with many contemporary solutions is that they make it seem that one has to battle one's way into this place of openness. There is no fighting involved, not for those who understand the tender secrets of human sharing that make all the difference in life. It takes trouble to be sensitive but it erases all the other troubles at the same time.

The Truth of Ourselves

Our ability to understand these depends, to some extent at least, on our capacity to live the truth of ourselves, to be ourselves gently and clearly in relationship to one another. Living the truth of our existence is not a simple or easy task. It is not being our sloppy selves or doing or saying anything we feel like. It depends far more on responding to our best possibilities, on realizing who we can be when we share our richness freely with other persons. There is a discipline connected with living the truth of our existence. It requires our best self-presentation, our strongest efforts to be everything we can be in relationship to others. It also involves our willingness to make room for others in our lives, to understand that the stage of friendship can never be occupied by only one person. It never works unless there is at least room enough for two and we must be as willing to make space for others as we are eager to have them make room for us.

What Can I Hear?

Listening is the key to the inside job of knowing something more about ourselves as persons. On that depends our understanding of the difficulties and challenges connected with getting along with other persons. By listening to ourselves we can focus on the internal aspects of our experience. Such readiness to hear reveals to us the answers to many of the other questions that trouble us. What can we hear that is true about ourselves? What, especially, can we hear of what is going on between ourselves and other persons? This latter question is all too infrequently placed by persons anxious to improve their human relationships. But it is the right question, and one that only we can answer. If friendship transcends external communication we understand it when we can actually hear what we are saying on all the levels of our personalities to others.

As we listen we begin to make sense out of what was previously bewildering. We make out the pattern of how things happen between ourselves and others. We begin to appreciate the role we play in the way things go between ourselves and others. We draw back from hurling the accusations that make everything that goes wrong in our lives the responsibility of those around us. We can hear, if we attend carefully enough to ourselves, the many ways in which we contribute to the way our relationships develop. We make our life histories far more than fate does. It is just that, focused on what is external, we all too often ignore the fact that we are a big part of what happens to us all the time.

Surprise, Surprise

It should not surprise us if, in listening and trying to get to the bottom of our feelings, we hear much that is unexpected. We may be threatened by some things we hear, delighted by others, and amused by still others. Life is suddenly richer when we open ourselves to the many levels of personality that lie beneath what we do and say on the surface of everyday life. We may discover, for example, that in certain relationships we are clearly meeting needs of our own that we may previously have denied or rationalized away. When we can be gentle and listen carefully we no longer need to be defensive because we are committed to the truth as it emerges from our inner selves.

Listening carefully we may also discover that we are quite often willing victims of the insults or manipulations of other persons. We may be surprised to find that we paint ourselves willingly into such corners. Yet only such discoveries enable us to do something about our interpersonal troubles. We should not think that we will discover only bad things. Listening to ourselves we are more likely to find a hint or two of unsuspected treasures, positive qualities within ourselves which we had not even permitted ourselves to see before. These could include generosity, compassion, tenderness, forgiveness, and other personal strengths that are indispensable to our efforts to improve our ways of getting along with other persons.

All too often we hide the best parts of ourselves, ignoring them or denying them, pretending, for example, to be gruff and self-sufficient when, in reality, we are neither of these. We may also discover that there are aspects of ourselves that need to be shared, that need to be incorporated into our relationships with others, that can be denied only at our own peril. We cannot, for example, refuse to share some of our weaknesses with other persons. They will be present anyway and enormous support derives from our ability to let people see what is unfinished about us. There is much to discover here, good and bad, but none of it is anything to be afraid of. The truth about ourselves makes us free of at least half the troubles of getting along with others.

What are We Doing to Each Other?

Once we have begun to listen and have developed a feel for our own style in regard to ourselves, we become more easily attuned to what we actually do to other persons in our relationship to them. What goals do we have in mind in our relationships and what needs are we meeting through these? Do we actively make room for others in our lives, do we allow them to be present to us, or do we keep them under fairly tight control, always holding off to a certain extent out of fear that they may find out something about us that we don't want revealed? It is also possible that we can treat other people somewhat impersonally while protesting that we are treating them with great personal solicitude. People do this when they decide to run the lives of other people. They have great self-confidence in their remedies. They have ideas about what other people can become and how they should behave. This is part of the do-gooder syndrome that is so destructive in human relationships. It is built, of course, on the do-gooder's internal need to do good rather than on anybody else's need to have good done to them.

Everyone of us should ask periodically: *What do I think I can do for others?* This would give us pause, make us evaluate our powers, and perhaps temper our sureness interfering in the decisions that are fundamentally the business of our friends, families, or neighbors. Can I really change other persons according to my master plan, whether this concerns a spouse, children, or students? Or is the most I can give them a fullness of my presence and a willingness to let them be fully present to me? This does not seem much to give and yet it is everything. What else can we do for each other except offer the gift of ourselves—that powerful and essential gift—to those around us? There is no way to supply an answer to this question. Better, however, to put this on your bathroom mirror than a prayer. It is a question that takes little trouble to ask and its answer can save us enormous trouble.

What Am I Doing to Myself?

Our lives have a certain shape because we want them that way. We may not immediately see all the reasons. They are not available at our conscious level of functioning but they are there inside us. We must take the trouble to find the answers for ourselves. What, in fact, do we do to ourselves in life and why do we do it? It makes no difference if our lives are terribly dull or crushingly overburdened with activities. Neither of these conditions would obtain unless, for reasons that only we can discover, we want it that way. Only in pursuing this question can we find out how we truly value other persons because the answer tells us how we value ourselves. What we do to ourselves, we discover, is also pretty much what we do to those around us.

Am I Ready to Change?

A troublesome question, indeed, but *the* question when we come right down to it. Am I ready to work at changing myself for the better? Unfortunately, many people look on time as something that should be quick-frozen. They are appalled to discover that things do change, that, for example, their relationship with their spouse progressively develops, in one way or another, from the first day of marriage all through life. They had planned, they say, on love always remaining the same. And yet it never does. That is because we change inevitably and relentlessly; we can grow in response to these changes or stand defiantly over against them. The latter path leads nowhere. We cannot preserve the moment. We can only continually enter into the future with other persons. Our only choice is to take the trouble to change. This willingness to change is our best guarantee that we will preserve and develop successfully our relationships with other persons. Getting along with others is a process. It does not depend so much on the past and what has gone before as much as it does on our willingness to move—and by move we mean grow—together into the future.

7

Problems with Sexuality

Human beings should never be surprised to be puzzled by their sexuality. Neither should they be puzzled to find themselves surprised by it. Sexuality remains one of the prime areas in which persons never get it all together.

It is an area in which people should be instinctively wary of reformers, experts, and preachers or all those who want to make political capital out of human sexual experience. Those who want to make a cause out of your sexuality give plenty of advice as they try to enlist you on their side in the sexual revolution. Most of the time, however, they want you to march in the direction they have chosen, to join in the battles that they have judged to be wise, and to engage in the behaviors they deem correct.

These decisions may not serve all people in a healthy and satisfying way. The odds are that such persons will—as most revolutionaries do—cause at least as much grief as happiness.

Sexuality is indeed a part of life in which people never get it all together, not completely anyway in sexuality; they remain vulnerable throughout their lives. Sexuality remains a dimension of life more appropriately approached with sensitivity and compassion than with loud noise and pompousness. We could use a little quiet—a moratorium on all urgings about what is right, good, or even playful about human sexuality—for the next five years. Many troubles would clear up in that time all by themselves.

We are emerging, like people making their way out of a house destroyed by an earthquake, from the wreckage of the sexual revolution. Are we wiser for what we have passed through? Line up some of the accomplishments that people boast about and one must wonder. Is it a triumph of maturity to have defended the right of free speech by keeping pornographic bookstores open and by encouraging the greedy makers of X-rated movies? Is human freedom exalted or demeaned by the proliferation of massage parlors and the freedom to shout almost any four-letter word but fire in crowded theaters? Will history wonder about what our concerns were when they study the energy with which we pursued the liberalization of abortion and the insistence that women alone should have control over their own bodies? We obviously need some perspective on these developments; one need not, however, apologize for doubting that they represent the highest point of human growth.

There have been distinct advantages in the human capacity to discuss sexual problems more openly and in the honest efforts on the part of scientists, philosophers, and theologians to learn more about and treat more sensitively this important aspect of human experience. We are entering a period of sorting out what has occurred, of becoming aware once more of the fact that human beings are not indifferent masses of neurons and bones and that there are consequences to the way they treat themselves and each other, that somebody always pays the price for the crusader's zeal, especially in an area as sensitive as human sexuality. It is better that all these things have developed. We can follow the Gospel maxim that we can allow all the plants to grow until the harvest time and then separate what is good from what is bad. But it is time to think about the complexities of human sexuality, time to define what we are looking for in life and what means we judge to be appropriate, in accord with our human and religious traditions, to achieve these.

People are just becoming aware of the fact that if one generation endorses everything which seems to eat away at the stability of marriage and the family, the next generation of confused children inherits a heavy weight of troubles as a result. After the great period of sexual freedom even some of those who have participated most ardently in it are beginning to wonder if, as writer Larry King remarked, "Maybe . . . people simply ought to be *better* than that. Maybe, by God, some things *ought* to be sacred," or, as he muses in a later paragraph, "One may find himself thinking, as William Faulkner said on completing his final novel, 'I've been meaning to quit all this.' Well, not exactly quit . . . Pause to reflect upon what all those years of tanglings and mixings have meant; and what has been gained or learned—or lost or forgotten—in life's many beds" (*Playboy,* December 1974, pp. 232, 234).

Is there a discernible pattern here, some design finally emerging from our headlong rush into sexual revolution and liberation? Who has been served by the victories gained in the name of freedom? Better still, what do people really want in terms of sexuality? Most Americans—one hopes most human beings—have had enough of this, enough of the sour unhappiness that invades the lives of people who have never been able to get their sexual experience into adequate human perspective and who have been misled by erotic gurus all along the way.

One of the troubles with modern-day attitudes toward sexuality—and one should not be judgmental but quite compassionate in reflecting on this—derives from the shallow philosophies that have turned into new imperatives concerning friendship, love, and sexuality itself. It is strange that in the era of women's liberation so many notions have gained widespread credence that have actually tended to strengthen the convictions or serve the needs of male chauvinists. These include the idea that people can do anything, "as long as nobody else is hurt." This is closely allied to the theory that anything is allowed "as long as nobody else knows about it." Perhaps one of the most dangerous and currently widespread adages, reflected largely among the young, reads, "Do anything that the other asks of you because this is what friends do."

This latter notion, prevalent on college campuses where young people are deeply interested in understanding the meaning of friendship and love, has led to further confusion rather than to enlightenment. Such notions, heavily romantic and immature, ignore the realities of interpersonal sharing, placing the uncompromised needs of one party always before those of the other and demanding what, in the eyes of those who champion this, seems to be heroic and loving sacrifice. In truth and in time this notion builds resentment and stores up unprocessed anger. What seems to be a noble commitment to the concerns of the other at any time and in any place—and is built on a willingness to give up totally one's own obligations and rights—has made both mischief and trouble for friendship. It also complicates the sexual bargaining that can be part of such a philosophy of life, especially at a time in which young people are still coming to terms with their own sexual identities. It is not the fault of the young that they have been overpraised in terms of their attitudes toward sexuality. They may feel more free and they may make very little of living together in arrangements that still astound their parents. The jury is still out, however, on many of these arrangements and a closer inspection of them reveals that they are not all poetic communitarianism nor progressive bohemian triumphs. In many situations, especially for younger people who are anxious to be accepted and who suffer enormously from the demands of peer pressure, they spend far more of themselves than they can afford sustaining these arrangements.

The fact is that human beings cannot live casually with each other as if what they did and felt about each other had no long-run consequences. The wounds are frequently invisible but it is doubtful that these arrangements, supported by philosophies that generally favor the man rather than the woman, are the solution to contemporary sexual confusion. They are merely another part of the problem. We can skip moralistic condemnations and still work for a return to commonsense thinking about what human beings are like and what values and experiences seem essential for them to develop a true appreciation of themselves and, therefore, a capacity to experience and share themselves in a loving and positive way.

Enormous harm is always done by those who want to use the sexuality of others for their own political ends. There is a wide spectrum of politically oriented sexuality present in contemporary America. Most of it is easily discernible. Extremists in most movements act out their own conflicts in the name of sexual liberation. These include, for example, the lesbian advocates who say that the best revenge women can take on men is to ignore them as sexual partners and to take themselves as lovers instead. There has been a new exaltation of masturbation as the only sure and satisfying means of sexual experience, one that leaves everybody else out of the picture. There is no discussion about the dynamic significance of such activity nor the isolating effects of such a viewpoint. There is just a multicolored world of sexual confusion that turns out to be as dazzling and as insubstantial as fireworks. Bisexuality is "in" according to certain faddish contemporary standards. People, even those who are bothered consciously by any major conflicts, are urged to admit their homosexuality, to come out of the closet and to give political support to what is represented as an alternate life-style. Such a confusion!

All that is lacking is someone with common sense to state they do not yet have all the answers to these issues of human sexuality, that we are, as a matter of fact, still more filled with questions than answers, and that the eager and unreflective promotion of this array of sexual choices may not be as prudent as some believe. One need not favor censorship nor Victorian attitudes to recognize that there are certain things about human sexuality that may be termed healthy and others which, despite their contemporary perverse glorification, remain unhealthy. There are things that can, without condescension, be labeled as immature, and there are other aspects of sexual behavior that can be defined as more fitting for mature adults. We are not helpless in telling the difference between those things which deepen our grasp on our own humanity and those which diminish it. We compound our troubles by thinking that everybody else knows better than we do about our own sexuality. The experts say: Broaden your view. The wise person knows that it is more important to deepen our view of sexuality. We can look within ourselves at least as much as we listen to the various apostles of extremely liberal sexual attitudes.

Human beings, trying to do the right thing with their lives, need encouragement and support to help them realize that their best instincts and their moral insights are not totally out-of-date, that profound human values are not to be treated lightly or abandoned quickly. Good people need reassurance that although sexuality will remain a source of trouble and vexation we can do sensible things to deal more constructively with it just as we can take healthy measures to avoid the excesses which confuse rather than clear up our difficulties. Among the principles that can be safely followed by those who wish to deal positively with the sexual troubles of the human condition are the following:

Accept sexuality in the context of human personality. Because human personality is intrinsically imperfect and therefore always unfinished, we should expect sex to be something like that as well. To anticipate that sexuality will be steady, consistent, or machine-like is to treat ourselves unkindly. It is to expect something that is not delivered in the human situation on any level. Sexuality, in other words, is like the rest of us, something that does not take care of itself and does not sum us up completely and is best understood in terms of our overall personality development.

A strange switch has occurred. A generation ago people were never supposed to admit that they experienced any doubts or uneasiness about their sexual identification. They were to hold firm and true, acting out the male or female role no matter what their internal experience told them. To deviate from this was to invite scorn, shame, and general social opprobrium. Now, however, we have come to a point where the admission of doubts and uneasiness is looked upon as a grace, that not knowing who you are or what you can be, and being ever ready to experiment with sexuality, is considered at least a small leap forward. This change from one extreme to another provides a perfect illustration of how potent social acceptance continues to be in the area of human development and expectations. To idealize either extreme is foolhardy, as it always is when we attempt to live up to the expectations that are designed for us by other persons.

It is a safe rule of thumb *not to try to solve our sexual problems on the basis of popular opinion, sophisticated practices, or the philosophies discussed on television talk shows.* It is wise not to accept sexual advice from anybody, physicians included, who seem more interested in selling their books than in helping human beings to understand themselves. It is always prudent to hold back from any ideal that represents a radical, absolute stance and that leaves little room for the flawed realities of the human situation.

We find our way slowly in terms of human sexuality, a day, a month, or a year at a time, and the journey has never been successfully plotted even by the most ardent social technicians. We need to respect our own personalities if we are going to serve ourselves well in terms of a deepened sexual understanding. The sooner we can live with the fact that we are never going to be perfect the more surely we will deal with our sexuality in a satisfying and enriching way. If we allow ourselves to be fallible and forgive ourselves and others for this, at least half of our troubles disappear.

Sexual problems are seldom helped by trying to solve them in and of themselves. Focusing too much on individual sexual problems distracts us from our capacity to understand and deal with our total personalities. We may be able to treat machines in this way, plucking out the offending element and replacing it, but we cannot do this with human persons. We human beings do not do well when we are treated as though we were an agglomeration of replaceable parts. The attitudes that we can have toward machines, from kicking them to turning them in, simply don't work well when we apply them to ourselves. We must treat ourselves whole or we will not treat ourselves well at all. We become a compounded trouble to ourselves because we have a completely inappropriate model of human behavior.

Our sexual functioning is related to the general level of our personality functioning. The best way for people to deal with their ordinary run-of-the-mill sexual confusions is to do something about themselves in general. They profit more by trying to understand what is good for them humanly than by trying to figure out what is good for them merely in a narrowly defined sexual way. There is a difference between emphasizing sexual and erotic experience and understanding these as essential and important components of our overall human experience. Troubles multiply when we overglorify the search for the erotic and when we make its achievement the final measure of our earthly contentment. There is more to us than the need for pleasurable experience. Pleasure does not, in anybody's dictionary, mean the same thing as happiness.

It would be naive to deny the fact that to seek erotic pleasure —sex without love if you will—is an immensely if temporarily satisfying experience for many people. Erica Jong, one of the writers from whom many "liberated" people are taking their current sexual cues, explains in her book *Fear of Flying* that women can be sexual roamers just as much as men. As a matter of fact, one of the troubles that bother people a great deal is their discovery of how selfish they can seem to be at certain moments in their urge for sexual experience. It can seem to blot out and transcend what they thought were fairly well-held convictions. It can blind them to the needs of other persons, reducing them to objects and finding one of the previously cited or similar philosophies as a vague kind of rationalization for the behavior. We should not, however, treat as a major discovery the surprising power of our erotic drives in an age that is heavily sexual and in a world where so many frustrations and disappointments force us in on ourselves. To find that we are capable of seeking pleasure instead of some richer or more lasting goal is merely one of the discoveries that tells us that we are human. It does not mean that we are a bold new generation of sexual adventurers; it does not mean we are terribly wicked. It does not even mean that we must necessarily give in to these urges. It suggests rather that we must see ourselves in overall human perspective, forgive ourselves for our feelings and for our indulgence of them, and then gently move ourselves back toward our best possibilities as persons.

Better for us all to be more patient with ourselves and, despite the glitter and glaring noises of contemporary society, to stand back and try to listen to the language of sexuality that is always telling us something about ourselves. It informs us, for example, that sexuality becomes a means for expressing aspects of personality that on the surface may seem far removed from it. Sexuality can be used in times of frustration and loneliness, as a vehicle for anger and retribution, and in a thousand not quite understood ways as an expression of unconscious conflicts and confusions. If we learn to understand this language just a little bit better, if we can grasp just a few more words and appreciate them, we will, like tourists who can at least get directions in a foreign land, be far more self-confident and far less alienated and panicked by what seems to be such a troublesome and assertive aspect of our personalities.

Somebody Else Doesn't Have the Answers

We may begin, even without the help of experts, to explore the meaning of our own sexuality. How do we perceive ourselves as sexual beings? Have we, for whatever reasons, separated our sexuality from ourselves so that it is generally regarded as a disowned part of us that is not integrated into our full sense of ourselves? Does it seem an alien force, something we try to ignore, or something we just adjust to the way we do a toothache or a noisy neighbor and never make fully part of ourselves? What does sexuality mean to us in our particular human identity? We may be able, for example, to identify those moments in which it is least a problem because I am most myself. These can be the self-forgetting moments of sexuality found in the context of a loving relationship. We may discover, most ancient and fresh of all discoveries, that if in our relationships with others we are reasonably well adjusted, if we are honest and open and try to be loving, then our sexuality is far less troublesome for us.

We may also discover that we are ignoring our sexuality, that there are aspects of it of which we remain afraid, and we may with profit explore these more deeply. Although professional assistance can be enormously helpful in this regard it is also possible that husband and wife can help each other greatly by developing a compassionate understanding for each other's uncertainties. Even here people may not ever get it all together but the trouble lessens notably when they no longer have to hide or talk only to themselves about their sexual worries. Quite ordinary people retain enormous power to heal each other. They do this by perceiving each other as total persons. When they love each other fully as human beings they are helping each other in many aspects of their personalities without even directly trying. A man and woman who love each other, for example, can chase away each other's bad dreams and wicked fantasies more easily than anybody else's suggestions or medicines. Love takes the cobwebs out of life because it gives those who love room to be themselves together. There are very few troubles that are not alleviated by the simple remedy of treating people as humanly and wholly as possible.

Adequate information about sexual functioning and sexual problems is also important. It is part of the way in which we treat ourselves as whole human beings. We do not try to operate from the heart alone; the intelligence must be served as well. We cannot survive old wives' tales or the strange collection of misinformation and rumors that still constitute the sexual heritage of so many contemporary Americans. Neither, however, can we rely on some of the philosophers of sex, such as the Playboy Advisor, who use sexual information to support their own not necessarily mature view of what life ought to be like. This should not keep us, however, from consulting those professional persons who have both a clear command of the current information about human sexuality and a mature capacity for communicating that to others.

There are, however, a number of fraudulent sexual therapists practicing in the land today and they make even the most reputable of them seem somewhat questionable. Persons should not hesitate to consult with medical and psychological experts but they should check out their credentials and their standing in the eyes of other professional persons. It is not wise to depend on persons who do not belong to professional organizations and who are unwilling to explain the nature of their training or to display their credentials. These persons are troublemakers and should be avoided at all costs. Many of these, barely beyond the amateur stage, set themselves up under vague titles that enable them to exploit human frailty and confusion in the area of sexuality.

If they are to be shunned, so too are the good-natured but muddle-headed people, whether they are general practitioners or pastors, who rely on outmoded advice when they are dealing with people with sexual difficulties. It is simple, almost fashionable, for example, to prescribe sex as a solution to marital or personal difficulties. This is usually in the context of telling somebody that they would be better off if they got married. As an example, this advice is frequently given to attractive and somewhat seductive-appearing young women who seem to have great sexual needs that are unsatisfied. Frequently this is the presenting picture of the hysteric personality, however, and to urge sex as a solution to their difficulties is to misunderstand that confusion about sexuality is part of rather than a solution to their problem. Being self-confident is no substitute for knowing what we are talking about in these matters.

Develop or intensify a philosophy or a theology of life. This sounds very fancy but it is one of the most helpful things we can do about the troubles of human sexuality. That is because sexuality is an aspect of human problems in general. Human beings need some vision of life that permits them to see a pattern or a meaning emerging from it. It is very difficult to live life in an absurd vacuum in which there is no connection between our activities and ourselves or between ourselves and other persons. Persons who lack an integrating philosophy of life are handicapped in dealing with sexuality because they are handicapped in dealing with life in general. A theology of life, however, directs us to a larger view of ourselves and of the events of our existence. It helps us to see ourselves whole and in relationship to history and to those who stand around us sharing life with us. Only we can resolve where we are going to stand or what values and meaning we are going to accept in relationship to the sacred business of human living. The fact that we are able to understand it as imperfect or flawed does not detract from but rather demands a religious explanation, and a religious explanation, despite the blunders of the centuries, does not blush at or look away from the sexual aspect of personality.

Nothing, in the long run, can be more healing than a sense of the religious significance of our lives and of the mysteries we make purchase of because of our own sexual experience. Genuine religious faith has an integrative role in our lives. It is ordered to putting sexuality back into a satisfying personal context. Religion that is alive proposes the right questions and offers a vision that enables us to find increasingly better answers.

Each of us must discover what we actually count as important in life. Do we want power, influence, or do we value love and relationship? Do we place the value of life and the uniqueness of human personality in the first place both in action and in theory? Or do we, as we sometimes can easily do, espouse the foregoing while we act in a fundamentally selfish and isolating fashion? Are we afraid of life or are we ready to take the risks that expand a sense of ourselves and our capacity to enter into it in a meaningful way?

What holds my life together? This is not a question for an abstract philosophical answer. It is a very practical one. What am I looking for and what do I try to get out of life? What gives my life its particular shape even if it is an inglorious one? Is there something I can do about this in order to break out of my self-concern or in order to become more sensitive and responsive to others? What are the obstacles, whether they are conflicts within my unconscious or obstacles in the external world that I allow to remain in my way? I can find out something about these things or I can go numbly along presuming I am driven totally and can take little into account of these powerful realities. What am I trying to achieve or to express?

Unfortunately, some people are just trying to pass time. That is why sexuality is a continuing puzzle for them and why they seem to settle for the promise of erotic deliverance rather than for a deeper experience of life. Can I enter into life more deeply by taking my own existence more seriously and by taking that of those closest to me more seriously as well? Do I treat myself like a whole person or am I still dealing with myself as an object or as a person that I faintly dislike with whom I feel uncomfortable? These are things each of us can and must do something about if we want to deal with our sexual troubles more effectively. *Do I think that as human beings we make more than just a passing difference to each other?* Do I have a philosophy of life that enables me to understand the accomplishments and disappointments, the tragedies and the surprises of daily life? Have I tried to understand those areas which, even though difficult to measure, are very real, those invisible areas between human beings in which they exchange what is richest and truest about themselves? The elements of this rest on whether we are committed to living the truth of our existence, on whether we are aware of this deep sense, on whether we have worked through the meaning of fidelity and whether we understand that such transactions are the most important in life and that they affect us whether anybody knows anything about what we do or think or feel about each other. It is very dangerous to feel that nobody else is ever hurt by what we do when it is clear that we can so easily and so often hurt each other without even trying very hard. Have we worked out some style of relationship that is respectful of those we love and which demands an adequate respect from them for our own rights and our own individuality? Are we rather captured by the utter romanticism of the philosophies that say that we must give in to the impulses and whims of others no matter what inconvenience this causes to ourselves? Have we thought about these things or not? Could we give an answer to a younger person presenting such questions to us?

Does sexuality take on some meaning in terms of the overall context of my life? Does it fit into my relationships, to my sense of myself even if only imperfectly? Or is it still a total mystery, a source of mystification and trouble, a presence within me rather than as an aspect of myself that I can experience and possess as part of my own identity?

When we ask ourselves these questions we realize that we may not yet have the answers. We also know that such answers do not come from anybody else, not from any sex expert or marriage manual. They are troublesome questions but they lead to the discovery of freeing answers. The best way, in the long run, for all of us average people to handle our sexual troubles is by learning to handle better our overall trouble of being human.

8

The Trouble with Marriage

What about marriage? Nothing has been talked about or worked on more incessantly than the modern American marriage. The reason is simple: As mentioned earlier, Americans want it, like so many other things, to work. They don't set out to get divorced. They want to experience a successful marriage. But successful marriage is a lot of trouble.

If it is perceived as anything but trouble, man and woman are bound to have difficulties living together and getting along in any kind of reasonable happiness. The notion that marriage solves life's problems, especially those of loneliness or of sexuality, is largely an illusion. Marriage doesn't solve anything. It is one long troublesome adventure that is at the same time filled with extraordinary possibilities for the peace and joy that all human beings long for. The big trouble is that joy does not come by itself nor is it marketed at a discount for those who want to avoid the risks involved in human closeness.

Marriage is a worthwhile kind of trouble to have because it is built on the efforts two people must continually make to stay in love with each other, to grow, and to give life to others. It is an institution in which people have the opportunity to realize the best and the richest truths about themselves and others. It is the institution in which human beings feel alive, that they have touched the core of existence and that they need not be afraid anymore.

Love, alas, is full of trouble; it is taking the trouble to work at love that makes the difference between successful and unsuccessful marriages. The most naive approach to marriage is that which feels that it will somehow take care of itself, that it is a special state that confers status, self-esteem, and emotional security. There can be nothing but trouble for people who feel that they have somehow entered into some science-fiction-like chamber where, living together, the world will bother them no more. It is good for married people to expect happiness but it is fatal to think that this is produced in any way except through their own steady commitment, working at life and its unpredictable difficulties together.

A simple but basic question that people who are married can ask themselves is: Do I want this marriage to work? What does it mean to me? Am I willing to pay the price to make it better or have things arrived at such a state that I am now adjusted to it or just used to it and don't care to do anything more about it? Good will is not enough in giving an answer to this question. We have to take practical steps to nourish and deepen the sustaining love of the married state. It requires us to do something as well as to think beautiful thoughts. It demands that we invest ourselves as well as say our prayers. It requires us to be able to meet each other freshly every day and to fight against letting life dull our responsiveness to one another.

A related mistaken expectation for married people is that their life together will always be like the life they shared in courtship and the early days of marriage. They are disappointed when this passionate, somewhat ethereal state begins slowly to disappear. That was what they thought was love and once it goes they don't know what to do about themselves or about their marriage. They are unprepared for the inevitable—that the way married people feel about each other does change steadily through the years. The most practical thing that a married couple can prepare for is change. The effort to remain the same, to hold things together as they were in some golden days of recollection is disastrous. That is to encourage a dreamlike state, to depart from reality and to live in contradiction to the laws that govern all other living things.

This is not to say that love disappears when it changes. It evolves and transforms itself, demanding something new of husband and wife, allowing them to discover things that they never suspected about each other and about the meaning of life itself. Marriage is a long steady journey and the learning that goes along with a man and woman living closely together is never ended. Their love can deepen and grow richer. That is change in a positive direction. If people are afraid of any change at all they reject the only one that is the right one for their pilgrimage together. Lovers have to give up what they have all the time. That is one of the conditions for deepening love, that people give up their adjustments in order to make newer and better ones, that they surrender their partially attained stability and throw themselves out of balance in order to be able to enter into life more deeply. Marriage is unsettling.

Marriage is filled with the glorious trouble of being alive. It is accepting this kind of trouble—and the changes with which it is filled—that allows people to know what it means to be human.

It is also helpful for people not to wait for something to happen to them. In marriage, as in almost everything else in life, if we want good things we have to do something about making them occur. We are called to be the authors of our own existence. Nobody is going to do it for us and there is no way in which we can tease a happy life out of the fates if we are unwilling to take responsibility for it ourselves. We design our lives whether we admit it or not. Waiting for some good fortune, or some change in one's spouse or some other stroke of good luck is a deadly passive stance for a partner who wants marriage to stay alive.

The trouble of marriage can be handled much more effectively if people perceive it as a fundamentally religious experience. Marriage has been described in terms of friendship, sexuality, and legal contracts. All of these have been invoked in order to give a more solid base to the life-style people set up together. What has been ignored, except by things like the Marriage Encounter movement, has been the powerful and helpful role that religious belief and tradition can play in assisting people to deal with the challenges and difficulties of marriage. This is because a deep religious view of life is an integrating force for our experience. It draws together a wide variety of human activities, puts order into them, and arranges them in a pattern so that they are no longer meaningless. Faith offers not only a center of gravity but a way of appreciating what takes place in life that interprets its significance and offers strong support to married people.

The trouble is that religion has at times been used in awkward and primitive ways in order to control and manage people. It has been used by joyless persons to destroy both marriage and the family in the name of keeping them together. Pietism is not the same as healthy religious belief. The resources of organized religion are enormous in offering a symbol system that helps people to identify their participation in a mystery that is greater than themselves. It gives them a way of viewing the sacrifice and demands of marriage in a Christian framework. It offers, for example, purpose to the kind of self-sacrifice that loving persons endure when they are trying to enlarge each other's lives. The Christian vision of marriage allows people to understand the general rhythm of their life as following that which is revealed in the life of Jesus. The themes of incarnation, death, and resurrection are actually experienced deeply by persons who are seriously trying to live sensitively and lovingly together. What they often need is a religious vision that helps them to identify what they are already in the midst of. They need not look outside of their life situation for the raw material for their active religious belief. They need not look on religion as something extra when they can be helped to see that their efforts to share their love with each other and with their children catch them up in the central dynamic redemptive effort that is proclaimed to the world by Christianity.

Beyond that stand enormous riches of symbolism, not all of which can be explained rationally to the curious intellect. Organized religion, in other words, does speak on several levels to human beings. It can reach the unconscious in a way that no other approach could manage. Religion takes people beneath the surface of their existence. It doesn't make everything clear but it helps people to live in the haze of life.

Unfortunately, many contemporary efforts to bolster marriage remain precisely at the surface level. That is the level at which people reach legal agreements about who will walk the dog and who will wash the dishes; these, of course, overemphasize the superficial qualities of their life-style. This is practically a national problem. People live on the surface, emphasizing the way they look and the things that they have and they wonder why they have so much trouble developing a better and deeper relationship with each other. This commitment to the surface is a symptom of the kind of narcissistic self-concern that makes it impossible for the individuals to break out of themselves and reach another person in a more genuine way. Living on the surface is the death, in other words, of what it means truly to be married to another person. An erotically oriented society, however, emphasizes surfaces above all else. This is an example of a disintegrated aspect of human experience. As such it emphasizes pleasures and styles that may be gratifying but on which a lasting marriage can hardly be built. They are probably not substantial enough to build a good affair on either.

The values of a religious faith that is mature, on the other hand, constantly refer people back to their inner experience while they also provide an array of insights and symbols which support and interpret the joys and tragedies of existence. People do not need religious leaders to tell them about the riches of their religious tradition. They can look more deeply into it for themselves. Indeed, a great many of the movements that have been most significant in offering nourishment to marriage have come from lay people who have had a genuine concern for incorporating the truths of their religious experience into the common day events of everyday life.

As elsewhere, it helps if people are never surprised by anything that is genuinely human. That includes seven-year itches, wandering eyes, and regrets about a wide variety of things. We should not be surprised to find that people who love each other very much can be distracted or that they can have bad days. The mistake comes when we interpret these as signs that our marriages are disintegrating or that we have become moral or psychological wrecks and that there is nothing left for us to do but to abandon the conventional ways of life for something new and more exciting. This is precisely what many people do in a society which, in general, looks on divorce as a solution to the difficulties of marriage. It is a divorce-prone environment and, while no one can argue the wisdom of recognizing marriages when they are dead and pronouncing them so, one must also hesitate to turn to divorce whenever there are tensions or difficulties in a marriage situation. Divorce has for some people become something to get, a fashionable thing to do, an experience that is inevitable somewhere along life's way.

A better recognition of acceptance of our human failings instead of a misreading of them as signals that we are tired of a particular relationship is essential for people who want to remain married to each other. The fact is that things don't just happen to us. We always contribute to their development. If a person begins to notice boredom, a need for a change, or finds that his or her toleration for flirting with other people is lowering, then it is time to examine the self. People sometimes engage in these kinds of tentative and mildly seductive behaviors because they enjoy the excitement involved in them. They sometimes do it in order to prove something about their own attractiveness to themselves. Many explanations can be offered for what is not an altogether uncommon experience for married people.

Husbands and wives should expect these things to happen and they should be prepared to withstand them rather than to play around with them as if they were of no consequence. When people get in trouble in these ways it is because they want to get in trouble. It is common sense—as old and clear as anything we know—that we can avoid these kinds of dangers to married life if we want to. Married persons must steadily explore their motivation for wanting to stay married and work hard at improving it and the practical decisions that should flow from it.

If we should not be surprised by anything that is truly human then we should never skip any occurrences that are really true, even when these may be hard to face. Confrontation is not the only way in which to deal with the truth of what is going on between us and other persons. There is a gentler way of facing up to the misunderstandings, disagreements, and imperfections of character that can be found in every married life. When people let the truths go by them, when they ignore them, or deny them even to themselves they build up a reservoir of anger that finally cracks through any dam of control and may wash away the marriage at the same time. Things that build up do not become dangerous overnight. They only acquire a devastating power when we ignore them or are afraid to face their implications.

As soon as persons experience something like this in their marriage they should bring it into the open, but savage confrontation is not the way to do it. When persons notice these first small cracks in the column of their relationship they can begin to discuss them with an awareness that they are dealing with fissionable material. Such small things carry a tremendous potential for destruction, and it is on these explosive snags that many a relationship has blown itself to pieces. The reason is that these small incidents stand symbolically for so much of what passes between a man and a woman. These small signs indicate what they really think and feel about each other. Into them are compressed a great many other aspects of their reciprocal experience. It is not a small difficulty to be shrugged off or forgotten. When these problems are discussed in a timely and understanding manner they can be handled with much greater ease and with far greater constructive effects. Taking the trouble to do this saves marriages from terminal trouble later on.

Husband and wife must be ready to understand each other in a practical way. Understanding that is built on our capacity to look at life from the viewpoint of the other is not an easy kind of gift to possess or give away to others. It remains central, however, to the success of any marriage relationship and it is crucial if people are to continue to work together on the troubles that face them regularly in married life. To understand another person is a continuing journey into territory that we have never really been in before. We do not settle for some conviction that we already know everything that there is to understand about the other individual; we never have them all summed up. A readiness to listen with understanding as the other reveals something of his or her experience not only helps people to manage the troubles of their own relationship but also deepens their experience of life itself. They can't be anything but better off after that.

Men and women must look at fidelity as something that is also highly significant in their relationship. The world has become careless about this in marriage and in other places. Fidelity, however, is an active dynamic reality. People work at fidelity all the time through their consciousness of and responsiveness to each other even when they are apart. Fidelity develops out of a willingness to live in a developing commitment to another human being, and there is nothing that is ever casual or without significance about it. Fidelity is not keeping an old promise as much as it is always discovering what is new and fresh in life together. Fidelity is built on the truth of man and woman believing in each other. Believers exchange extraordinary gifts in very simple ways. People who believe in each other have the capacity to give back to each other their possibilities. That is precisely the effect of an act of faith. Believing wipes away everything that is past and presents the person with a new chance for existence with no charges kept on the books against them. This is the living kind of faith that people who stay married have in each other and is the core of their dynamic fidelity. They know that what they do and think and how they act when they are apart has a lot to do with the vibrancy of this commitment.

People who love each other and want to deepen their marriage should avoid feeling like victims. They can do something even in the most difficult circumstances. Men and women are not victims of life and there are many practical things which they can do, many of them very small and simple, which help them to see the fresh possibilities that continue to reside in their life together. There are no tired old marriages. There are just tired and distracted people who have forgotten to look at each other and cannot remember how to look at life together. Perhaps the most central lesson for husband and wife to learn is that of respecting each other as separate, fully identified human beings. One can never live in the shadow of the other. One cannot be just the husband of somebody else or the wife of some other personality. That is not the way that marriages stay alive. People who love each other have to learn to let each other be, that is to have existences that are separate but in touch with each other. They have to free each other for that existence, letting each other go, giving each other room, not in some faddish open-marriage style that is built in insisting on one's own freedom but rooted more in each person's readiness to acknowledge the freedom of the other. This is not built on indifference but on understanding that a relationship remains vital only as long as those who participate in it remain strong and vital as individual personalities themselves. They cannot do this if the identity of one is absorbed totally in the identity of the other. It cannot and will not happen if one sacrifices everything for the sake of the other. It cannot happen if the relationship gets so out of balance that the identities become blurry. This is the hardest but most important part of developing a lasting, loving relationship.

Things to Remember

Husband and wife are wise to recall that their relationship is not a reasonable one. How often man and woman after a period of difficulty or strife approach each other with the phrase "Let's be reasonable about this . . ." and, of course, the last thing that married people ever are is reasonable with each other.

This does not mean that they are demented or stubbornly illogical; it means that their relationship is personal and is therefore one that exists on several levels besides that of intellect. To try to sum up a relationship as complex as one between two human beings who live intimately with each other in syllogistic form is to pursue an impossible fantasy. There is no way to be reasonable about something which is overladen with emotional factors and may, in ways we do not fully understand, be strongly affected by biochemical realities as well. One thing is sure: To try to be reasonable when we must, at all costs, be compassionately personal is merely to deepen the kind of trouble that people are already in.

Married people should begin to worry, as a matter of fact, if they have only logical problems to discuss. They should be deeply concerned if there is no overflow of emotion, no passionate concern about life or about each other. They should be properly upset if everything between them can be settled by the provisions of a legal document. That means that there is something dusty and drought-season-dry about their relationship. It might be polite, perhaps platonic, the kind of relationship one might have with a companion in the same classroom but hardly the kind that should obtain between people living intimately with each other. When passion is gone it is time for people to wonder why, to stand back and try to find out how their marriage became mummified.

Work at Developing a Sensitivity to Each Other

Becoming sensitive and continually understanding of each other requires concentration and hard work. It also requires that people do something concrete, each day if at all possible, to express this sensitivity and to show each other that they are actively seeking to understand and respond at more than a surface level. This is the kind of thing, for example, that is done with such success in the Marriage Encounter movement through the simple expedient of having husband and wife write each other short letters of concern and love each day.

A commitment to do this means that people, first of all, have to take the time to think about each other and they have to think about the things they love in each other. It is easy to forget to do this. Just remembering it a few moments a day and making it explicit by putting it into writing can make an enormous difference in developing one's sensitivity.

If one is not as sensitive to the other as is really desirable, then other things should perhaps be undertaken. An individual may want to read poetry, develop a deeper interest in music and the arts, or get some counseling that may help to attune him or her to the emotional factors in life. There are many practical things that can be done to increase the all-important element of sensitivity in a marriage.

Resolve to do something special for each other every day. This doesn't take much. It doesn't mean a big present. It means a little thoughtfulness. It means something done freely rather than out of obligation, something done out of regard for the other rather than out of any need or desire to manipulate the other. It should be the kind of thing that surprises the other with the message that they are treasured and loved for their own sake.

Do something different once a week and do it together. Do things that bring you into the realm of new experiences and break the grip of routine and dullness. The cost of these adventures need not be high. They are, in fact, priceless because they provide the kind of setting in which people can increase their respect for each other. Respect is used here in its original meaning. It refers to our capacity to look freshly at things. This is precisely what people caught up in the trouble of marriage must be able to do if they are going to give back to each other the possibilities of life. Looking freshly is an enormous aid to this. If people put themselves into a setting which is new it makes them look at each other from another angle. It can't hurt.

Stand back each day and view your marriage and your spouse

from a slightly different angle. Take a few moments in order to be able to do this. Shifting our angle of vision just a little bit gives us a measure of distance from our own perhaps prejudiced view and expands our capacity to understand and appreciate the best qualities in our marriage relationship. This can be done while one is commuting, while one is waiting for something; it can take place in any of the many extra moments that are so numerous in any day.

The Biggest Clue

Stop immediately and get help of some kind if you note a growing conviction in yourself that whatever is wrong is all the fault of the other party. As soon as we are sure that we are the totally aggrieved one, it is time to take a closer look at our existence with the other. No difficulty is caused totally by the other person. When we get to think that this is true, it means we are in more trouble than we think.

This is also true when we are totally surprised by a sudden difficulty which seems to have arisen from nowhere. Difficulties in marriage ordinarily come from inside it rather than from some distant place. When we are completely surprised we may not be paying enough attention to what is going on in our marriage. Before we harden ourselves in place by blaming everything on the other it is sensible to examine ourselves more carefully to find out if we have not played a larger role in this development than we suspect.

Sadly enough, many people do things to each other which they do not understand. They hurt each other when they don't want to. They separate when, in truth, they still love each other but when things seem to have gone too far or gotten so out of hand that nothing can be done but to move out of each other's range. There are many signals that occur before anything like this actually happens. Increasing our sensitivity to these possibilities enables us to make practical decisions about doing something constructive about such situations before they become critical. We can always do something if we notice what is going on in our lives. There is some trouble involved in this but it is nothing compared to the trouble it can spare us.

9

Threats

Who has not heard in an age of terrorism of threatening remarks and threatening letters? But the threats that really get us are the ones that we cannot hear or see at all, the ones scrawled not on the walls but inside our souls. These affect us on the unconscious levels of our human functioning and we receive their messages only in an indirect manner. Threats tumble into the caverns of the unconscious in disguise, toppling our adjustment on a plane we cannot rationally reach—so that we can literally say that we do not know what is going on. These threats, the bristling ends of which we experience consciously as anxiety, flow from psychological conflicts that are out of our range because they are out of our awareness.

This is one of the prime troubles of living, this nameless anxiety with unconscious roots. All we know is that we are upset, on edge, or as we often describe our puzzled selves, that we are not ourselves. Sometimes, instead of feeling anxiety, we notice —or, literally, do not notice that we use defenses to get through the days and nights of life. While those close to us can easily recognize our defensive maneuvers, we are usually the last ones to acknowledge them. Troublesome indeed and again because they are automatic and unconscious responses that handle the anxiety that springs from the various unconscious threats to our idea of ourselves. Psychological defense mechanisms manage the anxiety for us as surely as a Hollywood agent with a hot property. The churning negotiations take place down in the basement of our personalities while on the surface we employ a variety of defensive patterns that guard us from even the twinges of the underlying anxiety. The defense mechanisms, which include rationalization and projection, function to preserve and to enhance our idea of ourselves by choking off the source of the threat underground. They transform our perception of ourselves, plastering over our inconsistencies and sealing off the punctures in our psyche that would make us vulnerable to the waves of anxiety that would otherwise overwhelm us.

And where do these threats come from? We are threatened unconsciously by experiences that contradict or are inconsistent with a well-developed idea of ourselves. Some writers refer to the *self-concept* to describe our picture of ourselves. It takes the self-concept as the long-term product of a great many life experiences, especially those we had at very early ages. After a while this concept tends to harden and resist any modification even by the truth. We can maintain our self-deceptions through the array of convenient defenses that are available to us. They manage the inconsistency between what we perceive ourselves to be in our self-concept and what we are actually like in our genuine experience of life.

For example, individuals who perceive themselves as very hard workers will find their self-concepts threatened by an actual experience of disliking or avoiding work. That truth is literally too hard to face on a conscious level because acknowledging it would be ruinous to their self-esteem. The defenses are therefore immediately activated unconsciously and provide an enveloping psychological myth which we can employ to smooth out what would otherwise be a jagged rent in our psyches. Were we in this situation we could rationalize first-class evidences of laziness either by denying them or by distorting our perception of them so that they come out as evidence supporting our notion of ourselves as a zealous and dedicated worker. "I need to take so much time off," the rationalizer may say, "because I work so intensely that I get twice as much done as the ordinary person."

Such notions can work for any ideal vision we have of ourselves. A good wife, for example, will be under threat if she experiences a sexual interest in a man other than her husband. To face this directly would cause an upsurge in anxiety. The defense employed—projection to provide the idea that the interest is all on the man's part and not on hers—excuses her from the truth and enables her to live with a soothing and self-enhancing fiction.

Nobody likes defenses in the abstract but everybody uses them in the concrete. We employ them at least in small ways in order to cope with the varied sources of threat that exist most of the time for all of us who inhabit the human condition. We are all, after all, frequently inconsistent and we are not always ready to admit the truth about it. We patch things up—we tell little white lies or indulge in exaggerations or fool ourselves—and even feeble defenses generally work. Defenses become a problem only when they become a way of life. They can be identified by their hallmarks of denial or distortion and they only fool the person who uses them. They deaden threat and its end product of anxiety. Defenses are comparable to the drugs which professional athletes have been accused of using in order to deaden the pain in injured hands or legs. The pain is like the anxiety; it carries a message for us about something that is wrong. The drugs that erase the pain and allow the athlete to play in the ballgame do not protect him from the consequences of exposing an injured limb to the roughhouse of the game. Our defenses work in the same way; they make it difficult for us to hear the inner messages that say there is something wrong or out of balance inside us to which we should pay closer attention.

Threats are made on the unconscious level but we pay the ransom through the use of defenses on the conscious level to avoid facing what we are really doing to ourselves. We are often irritated when we are accused of being defensive and yet there is no way in which we can automatically rid ourselves of what is a natural inheritance in our human personalities. Unconscious processes do not respond to acts of the will. Defenses are, in fact, important and, when used in minor ways, they frequently gain us time in which to survey our situation and face the truth of life more clearly. Defenses help us to keep going in difficult moments. It is very hard, for example, to function adequately in an emergency situation without using the mechanism of denial. We have to shut off the threats in order to function effectively and we need not beat our breasts in shame because we employ these from time to time.

The trouble arises when we do not recognize just how we use defenses or do not understand what part they play in our lives. Troubles multiply when we consistently refuse to listen to our inner experience and prefer to distort it so that we can maintain a positive picture of ourselves and blame the world or other persons for our troubles. Using defenses as a major mode of adjustment constitutes one of the most crippling troubles that is known in the human condition. Using defenses this way interferes with personality growth and development. The defenses function protectively but they are always drawing the person into a smaller circle so that finally the individual is all alone there. The only view of reality available is filtered through a narrowed and closely defended space.

How can we tell if we are using defenses in a way that is out of line and troublesome for us? We answer that question by asking another: What do we do when somebody challenges a defense that we are using? It may be only in such a moment that we can recognize the fact that we are using a defensive maneuver. If we become very anxious when someone challenges some idea that we have of ourselves we have a clue that we are not really comfortable or at ease with our picture of ourselves. At some level we know that there are things missing, that there are things there we have not examined, carefully. If we feel guilty or become hostile when someone challenges our self-picture we also have undeniable evidence about our defensiveness. If we are, in other words, threatened when someone does not buy what we are selling about ourselves we are getting a message just as clear as that delivered by the pain in the athlete's body. Something is wrong and we have to look at it.

What threatens us? A great deal of the trouble of living could be minimized if we could get a better and more understanding perspective on some of the aspects of human experience that threaten all of us. These are the subjects that become taboo topics in a culture. We cannot handle them precisely because their exploration is too threatening to our familiar sense of ourselves. And yet most taboo topics center on some staple of human experience, something that everybody shares and yet nobody wants to take a good look at. There are things in every culture that are so threatening that we would be very anxious and ashamed if we had to confront our experience of them directly. And taboos survive even in a society that fancies itself liberated. These are hurts, real sources of trouble, for millions of persons. The so-called liberalization of society or the encouragement of people to act out their impulses does not bring relief. Understanding these tabooed dimensions of our personality, however, allows us to live far more comfortably and with much less trouble. These are not problems that people next door have; these are difficulties we all have.

Aspects of our human experience that retain their power to intimidate us include hostility, sexuality, and dependency needs. Despite the sexual revolution and the torrent of pornography that has washed across America many persons are still ill at ease with their sexual feelings. Many individuals report that they had a very restricted upbringing or that they were not given any information about sexuality or that the subject was treated with shame and anxiety in their own families. This kind of anxiety is, in a sense, catching. Despite the newly proclaimed sexual freedoms many people cannot easily or compassionately take a look at or listen with any comfort to their sexual impulses. They seem to them a tangle of forbidden and alien notions; their sexual feelings threaten them severely and they use defenses to avert their attention and manage their way through life. This inhibits their freedom and makes sexuality far more troublesome than it need be.

The same is true of hostility, a compound found in any strong feelings that well up in human personality. These are generally handled by repressing them as inappropriate except in circumstances where righteous anger may be indulged in with confident, clear-cut justification. It is very threatening for most of us when we experience anger at moments when we cannot justify it. And yet anger comes unbidden many times to all of us. It is not a mystery to be scorned but a reality to be accepted and understood. So too it is with our needs to be dependent at times. We never get over the need to be protected like children on certain occasions in our lives. Various cultural ideals indict the notion of letting ourselves be dependent by admitting that we need the protection or care of others at times; it is hard to accept this can be good instead of bad for us. Strong men, feeling that they must keep up their masculine front, for example, are made very uneasy by a periodic experience of wanting to be cared for by somebody else.

Others are threatened by tenderness because they think that this is an undesirable chink in the armor of their self-reliant personality. Still others of us are threatened by positive aspects of our experience. We are made uneasy, for example, by the discovery that we can like other persons and we have warm feelings for them; we tend to draw back and repress what can be quite wholesome reactions. It is not surprising to discover that many people repress some of the most admirable qualities of their personalities. They think that warmth and sensitivity are somehow inconsistent with what they would like to perceive in themselves. As a result, these good human qualities are denied or pushed out of the picture. Such qualities sometimes have to be loved out of people. It is not unusual for persons to discover and identify positive aspects of their personality only in the context of a loving human relationship. In a good relationship with another person they no longer experience threat; they no longer have to defend themselves because they are accepted as they are.

What can we do about the things that threaten us? We can set up with ourselves a more loving and acceptant relationship. We have to give ourselves permission to be human. This begins with a wiser understanding of our almost infinitely varied human capacity for reacting to life; we need a sense of the various levels—almost like geological strata—of our individuality. We are filled with reactions we might not choose to have in an ideal world. We feel impulses we wish we did not experience. We have fantasies that we wish we did not have flashing across our minds. Every human being experiences many feelings that he or she doesn't really want anybody else to know about. But that doesn't mean we are corrupt or totally shameful creatures.

We do not, for example, want anybody to know about the wide variety of sexual reactions we may experience. We do not even want ourselves to know. We think there is something wrong with us when, as a matter of fact, we cannot prevent ourselves from having these impulses. They can arise at very inappropriate times and can, therefore, be very threatening to us. And yet we need not act out these impulses. Nor are we their prisoners. We are not somehow wretched and perverted because we are capable of the diversity of human experience. We are simply human beings and we can distill the threat that causes so much anxiety by being able to accept ourselves as nothing more or less than that.

This is also true of hostility and the range of angry or belligerent impulses that can rise spontaneously in us. So it also is with the sometimes overwhelming feelings of wanting to return to the protected world of our childhood. We are all of these things at different times and we need not apologize for not being quite as antiseptic as, in some impossible ideal, we would like to be.

Accepting ourselves removes much of the trouble that is associated with the threats that produce anxiety in life. That is something we have to work at. It means that we need to take ourselves seriously, respect our own individuality, and not hurry to judge ourselves as evil or perverse. We must inspect ourselves forgivingly without feeling desperately alienated from everybody else just because we experience shocking or unusual impulses at times. Acceptance is built on understanding in a healthy way the complexity of the human condition in which we share. It helps if we are able to listen to everything that is going on inside of ourselves, realizing that the occurrence of feelings does not mean that these will ever be translated into outer behavior. We need to understand these things in context, in other words, if we are going to possess ourselves with the kind of dignity that is appropriate for mature human beings. A longer view of ourselves lessens our troubles immediately.

Listening carefully to ourselves leads us to naming our experiences correctly. This is the cutting edge of a healthy adjustment because it rejects the defensive position. Once we broaden our capacity to see ourselves we can more easily identify correctly what we experience even when this seems to be an inconsistent and therefore threatening feeling to our idea of ourselves. There is nothing wrong in admitting that we can have sexual or hostile feelings; there is no shame in realizing that we can long to have someone care for us every once in a while. There is, however, unending trouble in not making room in our picture of ourselves for these feelings. We may bind ourselves too tightly and sentence ourselves to the use of defenses in an unnecessary way in order to maintain our rigid functioning in life. Being able to accept and identify a wide range of our experiences defuses them and takes the threat out of them. We do not end up feeling that we are living with an attic filled with bats. We will understand that the human situation is the only one in which we can exist and that we have to accept and label correctly all aspects of our experience to know ourselves and take effective charge of our behavior.

This is a way of living out our truth more fully. We are not captured by our feelings and they have far less power over us when we can identify and live with them. We then have less need for denial because these elements, once they are identified properly, cause us less trouble because they no longer threaten us. And we walk much more surely through life when we are not ducking and dodging because of the rumbling threats within us. Facing all the truth lets the sunlight back into existence.

10

Feeling Bad

Guilt is one of the big troubles in life. When human beings experience it in an intense way, when it distorts their lives out of shape, it is not a sign that they are sinners but that they are in need of help with their emotional problems. Guilt comes into everybody's life but it usually comes in a smaller, less intense although very pervasive manner. We all know guilt at least in its milder form; it is not the major infection of serious emotional disturbance but it is toxic and it does interfere with our normal functioning.

We are all involved in coping with the problems of guilt—the trouble of feeling bad about life—all the time. We have no choice about this. We must deal with our guilt in order to keep going. Our trouble becomes complicated when we deal poorly or ineffectively with it. Our own reactions sometimes just make the trouble worse. At times we are manipulated by our guilt, forced into a corner by it, and we discover that both our freedom and our capacity to enjoy life are impaired. We try to solve the problem of feeling guilty but we do it in a way that is far more troublesome than helpful. Ineffective ways of dealing with our experience of guilt constitute one of the clearly unnecessary troubles of life.

Feeling bad, or feeling guilty, is a special kind of anxiety about our own behavior. This guilt, even in small doses, can powerfully control our behavior. We try to avoid the experience of guilt because it is so punishing. There is, then, a great reward in avoiding those behaviors which make us feel guilty. We are reinforced in these avoidance behaviors because they work so well. We stay rigidly within certain prescribed limits as though we were making our way through life on a path between stretches of electrified wire. There is only one road we can walk and we can stay on it, not necessarily because it is the right road, but because straying from it leads us back into the punishing experience of guilt.

It is not a bad thing to avoid evil, of course, but it is no favor to human beings to allow them to remain ignorant of its true nature. A healthy conscience does not keep a person out of contact with the elements of moral choice; it is not afraid of facing evil and understanding something of its nature. A healthy conscience is not a slave driver but a wise guide that allows us to live humanly. An obsessive and overcontrolled conscience forces us to live inhumanly, depriving us of joy, and, perhaps worse still, of the capacity to make mature moral choices.

We can tell the difference between an overcontrolled and a healthy conscience by inspecting their effects on our personalities. The driven conscience which mistakes puritanical propriety for genuine goodness maintains us as good children who are afraid to disobey. It keeps us at an immature level of development. A healthy conscience, on the other hand, frees us to grow humanly and to take on more responsibility for our own lives. It may lead us closer to the real face of evil but only so that we can recognize it and deal with it in a responsible manner.

A healthy conscience, then, directs us toward adult choices, toward a deeper awareness of our own responsibility for our lives and toward a feeling for our own capacity both for good and for evil. A healthy conscience assists us in achieving a deeper and wiser self-knowledge. This kind of conscience is not some laissez-faire mechanism, permitting us to do anything we feel like. It educates us to our choices and to their consequences; it instructs us in morality. One of the chief characteristics of a healthy conscience is that it does not do violence to us. It treats us humanly.

The obsessive style limits our choices to that band of activities in which we feel safe and approved, in which, indeed, we may feel saved for all eternity. Playing life safe this way keeps us from doing reprehensible things but it also prevents us from understanding the nature of life and the meaning of our own existence. It is more trouble than we could possibly imagine to try to lead a life that does nothing but avoid things that are wrong and that, in the process, prevents us from ever discovering what is right about ourselves. The obsessive style makes us more dependent on what somebody else says; the major characteristic of this attitude is the need for approval which those who experience it feel in their lives. Nothing that they do can have validity unless other authorities stamp it with their seal. This brings persons to undervalue themselves and to mistrust their own judgment, to throw away, in other words, the very aspects of their personality through which they define their moral presence in life.

The obsessive style also objectifies evil. It treats it as though it were something outside of us, something that can be avoided like plagues and the black lung disease if only we remain away from the environments in which these are common. Evil is much easier to deal with, of course, if we can objectify it and blame all our impulses on a devil roaming the world to tempt us. This may cause us, however, to overlook what goes on inside of ourselves, to blind ourselves to our own talent for mischief and our own at least partial inclination to evil. The mystery of original sin expresses an extraordinarily powerful reality: Human beings are capable of evil as well as of good. We are a mixed bag and we are notably deficient in self-knowledge if we do not take a serious look at the harm we can do to ourselves and to others. When we are blind to our capacity for evil we are controlled by it or we misname it and so misunderstand ourselves. This kind of conscience keeps us at a distance from who we really are.

An obsessive way of living does violence to us. When we are champions of the obsessive style we are very hard on ourselves and frequently just as hard on other persons. We cannot, for example, take a day off without working extra hours the day before and extra hours the day after. We have to pay, sometimes way above the market price, for the common experience of freedom. We don't feel right, we say, unless we do this or we claim that we could not live with ourselves. Such statements signal the trouble of a driving conscience. This attitude toward the self causes ulcers and heart attacks but its chief effect is the constant discomfort it causes the spirit. It is trouble twice confounded. We find ourselves locked into a way of living that is enormously draining and yet from which we dare not excuse ourselves for fear of feeling guilty about it. The obsessive attitude does violence to us by depriving us of the freedom to be. It estranges us from one of our richest and most enlarging capacities, that of being able to play, to re-create ourselves by being free at times to do nothing but to experience the wonder of life. There is little wonder available to the person troubled by an unfriendly conscience.

This unfriendly conscience drives us, at all costs, to do well. It forces people to succeed in terms of being approved by their teacher, their supervisor, or God Himself. Self-esteem depends totally on this approval. This is very harsh on human beings who, in the long run, must experience self-esteem as something that arises from their own worthiness. This obsessive conscience makes it depend always on a source outside us. Striving to be approved of also affects the way that obsessive persons perceive themselves and others. Other persons become either obstacles or opportunities for the obsessive person to use in order to gain approval in life. Persons are not perceived or valued in or for themselves. People are used, to put it bluntly but realistically, in order to advance a person's sense of doing the right thing. This kind of attitude, which is not deliberate, lessens our human ability to enter into and to enjoy human relationships. We must always get something out of them, ransom every moment so that no time is wasted or lost. Just relaxing in the presence of another person—just being with someone for no external reason at all—is beyond obsessive persons. Yet this simple experience is at the heart of a happy life.

Persons who are troubled even in a minor way with such a driving conscience do not solve the problem by intensifying their efforts to be approved. They do not escape the trouble by the inadequate solution of warding off the guilt they would feel if they let up for just a moment. They need to examine their attitude toward humanity in general and toward themselves in particular as a first step in freeing themselves from the experience of unnecessary guilt and the terrible trouble it causes in life.

We may ask ourselves whether we have become acquainted with—or friendly to—our true personalities. It is easy to have a surface idea of ourselves to think about ourselves as though we were some external object that could be evaluated and measured. But this is far different from experiencing our own humanity. We treat ourselves as objects rather than subjects when we always evaluate or look at ourselves from a distance. This is an operational way of dealing with ourselves in the third person.

But what is it like to be human? It is surely not to be perfect or to expect perfection in any of our activities. Do we give ourselves even a small break in consideration of this truth? Sometimes obsessive persons guarantee their own failure by setting ideals that are so high that they cannot possibly achieve them. They are always falling short and so they are always feeling bad. They feel guilty; this anxiety hangs like a fine mist over their lives and they can never disperse it because they can never find the solution to their agonizingly troublesome problem of trying to be perfect. Anybody who cannot settle for being imperfect is going to have nothing but trouble. The first step in being more human to ourselves depends on our understanding of the human situation, that flawed condition which we cannot escape and through which we must make ourselves present in life.

If we cannot settle for being imperfectly human we may ask

ourselves another question: What are we getting out of being so hard on ourselves? We never continue attitudes or activities that do not reward us in some way or other. Some self-examination may yield to us vital clues about why we are so unremitting in the demands we make on ourselves for behaviors that we can never in fact expect to achieve. Can we do without being so hard on ourselves? Most persons would say that they could but they don't know how. The answer depends on finding their way into what it is genuinely like to be human. This required some pause and some reflection, some compassion for themselves and some readiness to define that compassion operationally in their own lives. This attitude cannot be achieved overnight. It is, however, compatible with the highest ethical and religious teachings, with what the most humane philosophies recognize about persons. Driven individuals may need to take time to investigate the wisdom that has accumulated about the human situation. They cannot set out to master this in shorthand fashion; that would be typical of the obsessive style. A feeling for what it means to be human has to seep into us. The first step is to open ourselves to the possibility that we need not be perfect. The sense of relief that follows allows us to begin to become acquainted with our real identities.

It may be difficult to free ourselves or even to forgive ourselves for the fact that we must settle for a life in which we all make mistakes. This is especially true if our attitudes have been culturally reinforced. It is typical, for example, of Catholics who have been reared in a demanding cultural environment which put high value on avoiding evil and of conscientiously carrying out the moral dictates of the Church; they don't shake the excesses that may be involved in that very easily. We may, however, be able to get cultural reinforcement into perspective by standing at some distance from ourselves, by perceiving ourselves in the context of our life histories and thus thereby gain an understanding of how some of our exaggerated guilt was born. Intellectual knowledge alone is not enough to break the grip that these attitudes can have on us. It is, however, a beginning and it does give us some space in which to reflect more deeply on whether we need to continue in such a driven way through life.

Neither the Catholic Church nor any other Christian body expects people to be perfect. The sacramental life of the Catholic Church is built on an acknowledgment of the flaws in the human condition. It is meant to help us leap the gaps in existence. Some appreciation of the compassionate nature of Christianity helps persons to step away from a stance which they may have rigidly maintained for a long time. They may see that they need not demand from themselves what their authentic religious traditions do not demand either.

Beginning to trust ourselves is the important next step. This requires an emotional investment rather than just an intellectual judgment. It means becoming present to ourselves in a human way, forgiving ourselves for what is imperfect or unfinished about ourselves, and yet respecting ourselves enough to permit ourselves a little more living space. Morality only arises where there is enough elbowroom in which to look around and make decisions. Morality grows when people give themselves permission to live. A fuller life can start as simply as that. Obsessive persons may, for example, grant themselves permission just for an afternoon to be freer than they normally are. It can be put in the form of a permission or a pass. A person may only gradually be able to extend this permission to other days and times. Beginning in a small way to expand our life space makes the development of trust in our own selves a greater possibility.

The problem is that many persons have, in effect, institutionalized themselves. The institution is invisible, of course, but they show the classic effects of overinstitutionalization. Their horizons are limited, their capacity to enjoy life is impaired, and, in many ways, they need re-socialization in order to participate more in the activities of the world. A driven person can issue a weekend pass, realizing that it is not going to lead them to murder, robbery, or any other fearful assaults on the good order of society. Just getting out and away from the obsessive routine has the same effect as fresh air and friendship. We feel better. We can't quite tell why but we know that those things are good for us.

Obsessive people may also examine the nature of the things about which they worry. They are in trouble if they find that they are anxious about small things, so anxious, in fact, that they sometimes ignore far more pressing matters. The trouble with being obsessive is that it leads us to worry about the gnats while we miss the camels. It is a familiar problem, one about which Jesus spoke often. He wanted people to have a sense of values about what is important and what is not quite so important in life. His teaching has been perverted by those who have put everything into little things and who have missed the big things like love and friendship in the bargain.

Obsessive persons may also ask themselves whether the things that worry them are really likely to happen at all. It is characteristic of the overly conscientious to worry about things that never do happen. Again this distorts their focus, absorbing them with a world of unreality, exhausting them, and, in the long run, it does not have much meaning at all. They continually save themselves from things that never happen anyway.

The overconscientious—those afflicted with the trouble of constant guilt over everything in life—are afraid to use the freedom that is a necessary condition for their enjoyment of life. There is no easy way to get people to shift their sense of values but it may help if they realize that all their hard work tends to deprive them of what they want and need most, the simple enjoyment of life at first hand. They remain outsiders, settling for unnecessary trouble and remaining ignorant of the necessary trouble that is part of a happy life. They are so preoccupied with what does not count that they cannot come to grips with the things that do count and do last. What is the source of the fear that makes them hold back and hold on to themselves and things until they can no longer remember quite why they were acting this way in the first place?

When we remain locked up in ourselves we always make things worse. We compound our troubles even though we may think that we are fighting a titanic battle with the devil. Usually we are shadowboxing with ourselves. Unfortunately, people with an obsessive attitude toward their lives tend to fight lonely battles, keeping vigil against imagined evil spirits, wrestling like Jacob with the angel, with phantoms in the night. Remaining locked up—for example, staying away from people out of fear that they may lead us into evil—merely complicates the situation. The very thing that helps most is to get out of ourselves and to develop healthy relationships. These set the phantoms flying more surely than most pious resolutions. It is strange but true that the very things some people are afraid of—close relationships with other persons—are the very things that help them break out of this self-defeating pattern of oversupervising their lives. It works without a direct attack on the obsessive elements which is more like falling into quicksand than anything else. Human relationships, on the other hand, expand the whole personality and help the person feel better because they help the person to grow. The fears fall away of their own weight.

A false conscience is as dangerous in its own way as no conscience at all. Neurotic guilt—unnecessary broken-field running through life to avoid what is evil—can blind us to a sense of real guilt about things over which we should experience some anxiety. In other words, this continual worrying about small deals may blind us to an understanding of the big deals in life. Ruminating about what is unimportant makes it difficult for us to grasp what is truly important. We can only experience real guilt if we know who we really are. We have to clear away the clutter of unnecessary guilt in order to recognize the face of genuine guilt in our lives. Real guilt is appropriate but the trouble of obsessive fear makes it more difficult for us to appreciate it.

A capacity to experience genuine guilt depends on our understanding our own identity. It also depends on our discovery of the truth of our religious and cultural traditions. We cannot be guilty if we have a false sense of what guilt involves. We cannot experience real guilt if we think that it only involves things outside of ourselves or that it is tied up with minute regulations or the obsessive need to avoid dangers. Healthy persons feel appropriately guilty when they transgress in a serious matter in life. This means that they act in and through their own person, make a choice not influenced too heavily by emotion—that they know what they are doing—and go ahead and do it anyway. Sin is a personal act; it demands our complete presence in life. Sin is not a distraction or something equivalent to neurosis. It is rather an intensely human activity. We can only commit sin if we understand who we are and live deeply enough in that identity to stamp our own brand on our choices.

A developed sense of morality—an understanding of our genuine troubles—depends on our willingness to acknowledge the truth about our choices and our actions. We must see ourselves in context; we never live cut off from other persons. We leave marks on them all the time. Nor are we indifferent in what we think or feel or in the ways we behave toward each other. Much of what is most important in life is invisible; it takes place in those spaces between ourselves and other persons. We really can do things to other persons; we can hurt them or use them selfishly, and we can do these things deliberately. When we can acknowledge these we feel an appropriate guilt because we know that we have lost some of our humanness in the activity. This is not child's play; it is substantial human activity and we can do something about it.

It is not enough, of course, just to experience guilt over the ways in which we may offend other persons. We must also be able to deal with our guilt and this depends on our ability to acknowledge that we have a capacity for doing evil, that sin proceeds from us rather than from outside of us. We can only forgive ourselves and reincorporate ourselves into the human situation if we face these truths about ourselves. There is something therapeutic in a willingness to acknowledge what we do wrong. That is the genius of the sacramental notion of penance. It requires us first of all to face ourselves and to acknowledge our own guilt and then to verbalize it, to externalize it so that we can free ourselves from its choking grip. The absolution given by a confessor follows on the absolution we give ourselves. We have to be adults to be sinners and we also have to be adults to forgive ourselves. Life may consist in a long series of experiences in which we grow fuller and wiser because we are able to process our good and evil humanly. It is a human thing to do wrong; it is a profoundly human and enlarging thing to admit it and to heal ourselves with forgiveness and to reinsert ourselves more deeply into our life situation as a result. We eliminate much of the unnecessary trouble of life when we can distinguish between real and false guilt. It is much better to live intensely enough to experience real guilt than to stumble through existence weighed down by the chains of neurotic guilt.

11

Feeling Sad

Sadness, like the bond in good paper, is a mark that is found in the very texture of the human condition itself. There are dregs in the cup life offers us to drink every day. We cannot escape sadnesses, large or small, except by breaking out of life altogether. Life and death, love and hate, joy and sadness: These experiences are constantly intermingled in our existence. We cannot pull them apart without destroying the meaning of life itself. One is reminded of the answer Pope John XXIII gave when asked why he had called a General Council of the Catholic Church. "To make man's sojourn on earth less sad," he replied. A man wise enough to know that he could not end the sadness of the human family, this good Pope was also compassionate enough to try to eliminate unnecessary sources of suffering.

Sadness comes in many sizes but it comes all the time. We need to understand the various dimensions of this experience and also accept some of the ground rules that guide us in trying to manage this trouble more humanly in our own lives. First of all, nobody can take sadness out of our lives. Neither can we eliminate it from the lives of others. We can lessen it and be a source of strength in assisting people to deal with their own sadness but there is no way to uproot it completely. Secondly, we cannot escape sadness although people attempt to do this all the time. We can anesthetize ourselves to it but it waits for us anyway. Sadness is a very patient phenomenon. Thirdly, we cannot ignore sadness or pretend that it doesn't bother us. Coolness or detachment may be a final apathetic stage in a reaction to loss or deprivation. It is not, however, a good way to handle depression or grief in the long run. We cannot sit as though we were unperturbed by the rumblings in our own unconscious. Fourthly, we need to face sorrow, accept its inevitability, sort out what is necessary from what is unnecessary and try to understand it as deeply as possible.

We need to set it in a wheel of meaning so that we can see it in its relationship to the other events of life. We must think about it, meditate about it, and pray over it. We need a mature attitude toward sadness and we only acquire this when we are able to face it, not to stare it down, but to learn to live humanly with it as a presence in our lives. This is related to the acquisition of wisdom, maturity, and is strongly influenced by our vision of the religious meaning of existence. We are always processing the sorrows of life, working them out, trying to get a more balanced view, a feel for this phenomenon that is never very far from us. Loss, separation, and varied hard knocks of life all tend to throw us off-balance. That is why we keep working at it and why we never achieve a final solution. Our own growth as human persons is our best achievement in our efforts to see sadness in correct perspective.

What can we understand about the various phases of sadness in our lives? We begin with the gently shifting moods that are always with us. We will never understand everything about our moods, although we can learn to take them into account, and to respect them for the effect they can have on our decisions and behavior. We should not be surprised by our moods or frustrated unduly when we cannot track them down. They are frequently the products of unconscious processes of which we can never become fully aware. They are the prevailing winds of our lives, however, and some self-observation can save us from making things worse, making others bear the brunt of them, or acting too precipitously under their influence.

We can also understand the difference between a deep sadness in a serious depression and the kind of sadness that we experience in brief reactions. These are both painful but they are very different. So too is the kind of depression that is the secondary phenomenon in certain illnesses. It is not unusual, for example, for people who have suffered a heart attack to experience a concomitant bout of depression. The depression is not the main problem, although it must be handled, and we are wise when we recognize those situations in which such depressions are likely to appear.

A deep melancholic depression differs from grief in the fact that when we mourn we do not feel worthless. When we are in the grip of depression we do. As Freud himself wrote, "In mourning it is the world which has become poor and empty; in melancholia it is the ego itself" (*Mourning and Melancholia,* 1917, p. 246). The period of acute turmoil is much shorter in grief reaction. It is, as are many other situational depressions, self-limiting. A serious depression is more like a chronic condition. It resembles an illness and involves psychosomatic reactions and may well incapacitate persons in their personal and professional lives. A serious depression of this sort needs professional treatment. A grief reaction needs time and the shared humanity of others.

Most of the garden-variety bad moods that we experience are related to some kind of loss, separation, or disappointment. The grief that goes with mourning follows on the loss by death of a loved one. There are, however, many minor losses that can affect our general tone of well-being for good or for ill. These are different orchestrations of the same theme of loss or rejection. Sometimes depression seems to come over us very swiftly, as though some gear had suddenly shifted in our souls. It is not a mysterious overtaking of us by an enemy, however, and we can usually relate it to an event in our everyday lives.

We are speaking in this chapter of the milder experiences of depression which we all know well. What we frequently do not realize is that there are ways in which we can listen to our experience of depression and trace it down to uncover its source. Understanding depression in this way is one of the best means we have both of treating ourselves humanly and of freeing ourselves of the effects of the depressive episode. There are many things, in other words, that we can do something about. We need not just hang on until the depression passes. Nor do we just have to pray for relief. We have other options which we can exercise. We can begin to question ourselves rather than just surrender to the storm of depression and then wait until it blows itself out.

We may begin, for example, with the question "What have I lost?" It is obvious in a grieving situation that the loss is that of a spouse or a close friend or family member. The smaller losses of life are not, however, so obvious. We do not know what we have lost or we feel that to admit that we could be affected by some of the things which, in fact, do depress us would reveal us as small or petty individuals. This is another clue to the fact that our self-esteem is involved; our self-esteem is on the line in life almost all the time. We can be depressed, for example, when we hear good news about somebody else. There is often an implicit loss of self-esteem in the good fortune of others. We deny that we feel the way we do but that does not change the situation. We may use a defense, keep up a good front, or try not to let our depressions show. That does not alter the basic situation one bit. When we admit that we experience such feelings we can free ourselves both from these emotions and from our depressive reaction to them.

At times it does not take much to pull the props out from our self-esteem. We can be affected by minor incidents, by things as small as unreturned telephone calls or things as big as being passed over for an important social invitation or a promotion at work. Great disappointments that are painful experiences of rejection can coexist with minor ones; they are on opposite sides of the continuum but they are both experienced as rejection. In the everyday, garden variety of such black moods, pursuing the question "What have I lost?" leads us back toward the light. When we find what it is we have lost we can sometimes smile at ourselves, a compassionate forgiving smile that lifts the depression and gets us back into life.

A closely related question that we frequently do not ask, even though it seems obvious, is this: "What stress am I under?" We are sometimes in the midst of very stressful situations and we are so defended by denial against admitting their effect on us that we cannot make the connection between an experience of depression and the stress itself. Stressful circumstances precipitate depression. They do this because they make us more vulnerable to the incidents in life that have the potential for depressing us. The discovery that we are under stress enables us to see ourselves in a better perspective. We can also stop tensing our muscles and give ourselves a better break. We can shield ourselves from unnecessary sadness by taking some precautions that are simple but effective. We can avoid, for example, adding other stresses at an already difficult time in our lives. We can avoid seeing people or doing things which cause us serious stress. We can anticipate and plan our lives a little better.

A further question that is significant in this area asks us, "What am I angry about?" The classic psychoanalytic formulation about the cause of depression suggests that it is often the outcome of anger which we experience toward others but which we cannot admit or express directly to them. Because we cannot do this we turn it toward ourselves and depression is the result. Depression, in this understanding, is inverted anger. The exploration of what we may really be angry at can free us from having to be angry at ourselves. There are many possibilities involved in this. We are sometimes angry at persons we love but we cannot face this in our awareness. It violates what we want to feel toward them all the time and we are afraid that even a small deviation from this positive emotion would be disastrous. We may be angry toward somebody who has power over us and so we are intimidated and are left only to turn the anger inward toward ourselves. Reflection on the way anger that is ignored or suppressed can work its way blackly into our psyches is one of the most constructive ways in which we can treat ourselves humanly.

We may also ask, "Am I falling short of my ideal?" Clearly, this is related to some of the circumstances revealed by the previous questions. When we disappoint ourselves, however, by not seeming to live up to the ideals we have sketched out for ourselves, we can react by becoming depressed. Frequently the ideal we have for ourselves is unrealistic. Merely to feel sad about something about which we could do something constructive constitutes unnecessary roughness on our own persons. If we find that our depression is related to an ideal we cannot seem to attain, then it is time to explore our identity to see if we have a realistic grasp of ourselves. False ideals often spring from false perceptions of our own selves. If we correct our idea of ourselves we also necessarily redraw our ideals. Things get into line in a more realistic fashion. We achieve our modified ideals more successfully and eliminate the disappointment as a source of possible depression.

Other formulations about the genesis of depression in our lives lead us to ask, "Am I helpless about some situation in my life?" Closely related to this is the inquiry "Am I hopeless about something in my life?" Is there some situation about which we feel powerless? Is there some situation where we have thrown in the towel, in which we no longer think that we can achieve anything at all? These are killers of the spirit and depression is our reaction to such feelings of helplessness and hopelessness. As in other situations, however, we sometimes do not realize that we are experiencing a feeling of helplessness or hopelessness. We do not let ourselves see that and so we shield ourselves from the information we need to discover the real roots of our depressed reaction. It is not easy to admit that we have given up on a person or a problem—or even a lifework—but to accept the truth helps us to understand and deal more effectively with the depression.

Many people expect the worst to happen. They have a permanent negative set toward life. We may well ask whether we are inclined to look at life pessimistically. Are we indeed those who can always see what will go wrong with the projects of life? Are the possibilities always threatening as far as we are concerned? These may be clues to an attitude which can be very destructive of our human spirit. This negative thinking, according to some theorists, leads to a negative emotional tone and, therefore, a generally depressed presentation of the self in the face of life. There are no easy ways to surmount this but the discovery that we have a hand in shaping our own black moods may be a great help to us in examining and ridding ourselves of negative thoughts. Positive thinking is not just a shallow technique advocated by Norman Vincent Peale. Even to stop expecting the worst is a great deal better than the usual stance of persons enamored of Doomsday.

"Have I learned to be helpless?" This may seem an unusual question and yet some people learn a style of relating to others that is an operational definition of helplessness. Some people settle for a passive stance in the face of life's frustrations and challenges. They see no relationship between what they can do and the lifting of the depression that settles on them when they are in this passive state. We can learn this pattern and never quite realize it while we are doing it. The depression seems a mystery until we see that we choose helplessness in certain circumstances. We cut our life's possibilities off. We fail to believe in ourselves in a certain way and this brings on a depressed mood. There is certainly plenty we can do about it once we identify it. We are limited only by our imagination. If we hold on to our neurotic learning, however, and remain helpless we are not treating ourselves humanly or respectfully.

Have I acquired a sick role, a dependent role that depresses me and yet enables me to manipulate other persons? Do the rewards, in other words, that go with being down make up for the depression itself? Do we use depression to attract attention, gain sympathy, or to get people to do things we want them to do? It is behavior as old as the race and it is not so utterly mysterious that we cannot identify it and do something about it.

Just as important for us in handling our everyday moods and bad spells is an examination of our characteristic way of handling them. We may discover, by asking these questions of ourselves, that we have never really looked very closely at our style of dealing with depression, that we have always just put up with it or waited for it to pass. We may find out that we do not have to keep using techniques which merely impact our depression. Denying it, turning aside from the help of others, going off by ourselves—these are all ineffective ways of dealing with depression. So too are the use of drugs or alcohol or the effort to engage ourselves in busy work or in some other trivial but distracting occupation.

Our general style in life is revealed in the way we deal with our depressions. They are an occasion for being gentle and understanding with ourselves and for treating ourselves more humanly. We can go a long way in understanding ourselves, in possessing ourselves more deeply, if we identify rather than hide the factors that cause these moods to come upon us. We are not helpless nor are we hopeless. We can, especially in the context of a mature view of life, explore and overcome many of the sadnesses of existence.

Grief associated with mourning is a very different situation. There is a work involved in mourning, as Freud observed, "grief work" that follows on the loss of a loved one. Much of this is done unconsciously and symbolically. It is not a rational or an easily analyzed phenomenon. We are helped immensely, however, when we can appreciate the complex nature of the mourning process and when we can give ourselves the freedom to mourn and not feel that it is a weakness or that it is an indulgence that we must deny ourselves.

The work of mourning is precisely that activity through which the individual readjusts to loss in life. He or she emerges (the loss dealt with at the end of the mourning) and is able to get back into life itself. After the initial pain and numbness there is frequently a period of symbolic search for the lost person. Sometimes strange and unexpected kinds of behavior develop; some persons suddenly experience sexual problems they never had before, but these must be seen in the context of the overall shift in dynamics that is taking place. Mourning is hard work and nobody can take over and do it for the grieving person. Those who interfere or try to distract mourners do them a disservice. Those who jolly them along interfere with the work that mourners alone can do. We can offer substantial support to people through our understanding presence in their lives but, in the long run, we have to respect them enough to allow them to work through their grief for themselves.

It is possible for persons to anticipate some of this grief and work it through in advance. Such an approach has been suggested for couples when one of them is terminally ill. Instead of pretending that nothing is wrong they can realistically share what they are both feeling deeply. This anticipation becomes an intense experience and does seem to help lift away the depression.

It is most important to use our wits against the forces that would rob us of joy in life. We are not helpless and some compassionate insight can free us from the sadnesses that are unnecessary so that we can deal more humanly with those that are.

12

Boredom

Boredom is currently a very interesting topic. Americans, in typical fashion, look on it as a problem to be solved. They have already put enormous energy and ingenuity into eliminating it the way they have eliminated infectious diseases. Indeed, one of the reasons boredom is written and talked about so much is that it offers us something different; it is not boring to read about boredom. Well, what about boredom? It is a trouble everybody has to face. What can we understand about it and what can we do about it?

Is boredom just the problem of assembly line workers, men and women who must repeat the same task over and over every day? Or is it a problem of the eventual sameness of life, the by-product of routine? Is boredom something that is essentially an enemy of human beings, something we must be cured of, a problem that must be solved? It is possible, after all, that boredom has more than one face. We can mean many things when we speak of boredom; if we are going to deal with it in our own lives we have to understand what we mean when we talk about it.

It is even possible that there are positive aspects to the experience of boredom. Feeling bored at least tells us something about ourselves, something that we might not otherwise know. Boredom is informative in certain situations if we are attuned to catching its signals. It may, in fact, lead us to achievements or insights otherwise unavailable to us. Boredom can also have a religious significance, a philosophical meaning, because its experience challenges us to examine the way we look at life and its significance. Boredom may result from a diminished sense of meaning, an impoverished symbolic sense about existence.

"The blue collar blues," it has been called, or "the white collar woes." This phenomenon has been described often enough. There have even been numerous experiments designed throughout the world to counteract the dulling effect of the assembly line. Jobs have been broken up so that a team of workers may participate, for example, in the total construction of a product like an automobile from start to finish rather than on just one aspect of it. There have been experiments in doing without the watchful eyes of the foreman, allowing teams of workers to set their own goals and to have greater decision-making power over their work. Many of these efforts are designed to increase productivity while lessening boredom.

This is a classic kind of boredom and much energy has gone into its solution because of its practical economic consequences. When we have to pay for being bored we quickly do something about it. The stiffening effects of a recession have lessened the complaints about boredom by assembly-line workers who have been fortunate enough to retain their jobs. Much of it depends on the times, on the amount of fat in the economy and the amount of leisure time available to workers. Powerful external conditions, then, alter our perceptions of what is boring or not at our work.

Boredom on the job is, unfortunately, far more widespread than just in automobile plants. According to Studs Terkel's book *Working,* most people are unhappy at their work. They have chosen it in order to make money and to make a living far more than to express themselves. They put up with it for practical purposes but they do not find that it engages their personalities or helps them to experience life more fully. This may be a function of the kind of values that have been presented in our society or evidence of the guide limitations on job change that come immediately into the lives of people who must support themselves, their parents, or their own family. Not everybody is free, in other words, to change jobs easily. We are all vulnerable to boredom, no matter what our work is, but we are not victims if we can reflect on and perhaps modify some of our attitudes.

We can begin, for example, by examining our attitudes toward life itself. Are we expecting it to be the way it is on television programs or in the movies? Or do we have some appreciation for its routine nature? Even the most interesting of work has routine aspects. There is no escape from what is repetitive and dull. We may need a way of seeing ourselves and life around us that will help us deal more constructively with what we cannot ever totally escape. We may have to examine our own work and life expectations.

If we try to discover what people do all day we would probably come up with the answer that they don't do very much. Life seems to be filled with blank spaces, waiting, and looking forward to the future. People look at events, graduations, trips, and other social affairs as anchors that enable them to ride through the dead and unmoving seas of their other long days. Life depends, for most of us, on the energy and meaning enclosed in and through our relationships with each other. When these are deep enough they can hold us together, deliver to us a sense of ourselves, and allow us a vision of the world that enables us to discover the small sources of wonder that refresh us and keep us going. A capacity for loving is closely related to that for working. To fail to work at discovering the magic that resides in ordinary experience leads on to crushing boredom.

Many people try to solve the problem, not by discovering the deeper layers of their own existence, but by searching for excitement or diversion. The pilgrimages to various ecstasies are numerous. They are sold in *how to improve yourself* books, in the wonders guaranteed at various centers for personality change, in the baths at Esalen and in the vague promises of singles' cruises. People function better when something big is going on. As Rollo May has observed, many soldiers who participated in the fury of the Second World War returned to routine jobs and looked back at the terror and excitement of battle as the most meaningful period of their lives. There is some evidence to suggest that people's mental health improves when they live in the stress of wartime conditions. There is less depression in tense Belfast, for example, than in the neighboring, peaceful County Down.

We cannot, of course, have wars merely to provide the excitement that fends off boredom. There are some who theorize, however, that it is precisely our need for intense stimulation that leads people to violence, to settling things finally by the fierce and exciting conditions of total war. There are lesser things, some of them carrying negative consequences for human beings, in which they engage in order to break the boredom of life. These are events which, as Studs Terkel observes, "make the day go faster." They include gambling, playing the stock market, engaging in life-endangering recreations, and so forth.

The trouble is that, sooner or later, we all have to go back to ordinary life. We can visit Las Vegas for the gambling or a shrine to seek a cure but we can't stay at either place forever. Pilgrimages are only made—to whatever destination—in order to enable us to return home again. We go out to the desert, or to the mountaintop, not to stay there but to develop the kind of perspective that enables us to see our own ordinary lives more clearly. We may buy some time or some thrills but we do not solve the basic problem of the ordinary nature of our lives.

It is also true that life is hard. That may be what makes it boring to some people who are incapable of opening themselves to its real challenges. They do not try to develop their human relationships, they do not try to express themselves in their own work; they sail along on the surface creating their own boredom because of their reluctance to get any more deeply into life itself.

We might include among these those who affect boredom,

who make it a life-style that mocks the ordinary existence of good people. It is a faintly decadent pose that can be noted in the lives of some celebrities. There is, for example, the Hollywood star who, in answer to all questions, replies that everything is "such a bore." Andy Warhol, for example, says, "I like boring things" and delights in having his films called "Super bores," examples of what he terms an "aesthetic of boredom." He is cleverly putting society down, of course, and no doubt finds that the financial rewards of his pose are far from boring.

Such a style, however, while mildly entertaining to the rest of us, represents a retreat from life and a hostile rejection of the way everybody else has to live. Boredom may reflect a lack of capacity to invest in others; it may indicate unwillingness to invest in others. It is through these techniques, through the life-styles that are endlessly described for us on talk shows, that life is made into a cruel game by shallow persons who look down at the public but take its money. Worshiping the superficial is a fairly popular activity, however—there is a lot of it going around. People with only superficial entertainments have little left if they are deprived of these glittering objects. Boredom as a sophisticated life-style may be the best that some people can do about living in general. It is hardly, however, worth imitating.

The feeling of boredom may be, in some instances, evidence of underlying emotional pathology. Some people spend their whole lives trying to suppress a dangerous impulse that lives at an unconscious level within them. They may be successful but they pay for it in their failure to develop their total personalities. They seek for distractions but they are always absorbed in keeping this unconscious threat under control. As a result they do not feel free to invest themselves easily in others. Neither can they carry out projects very spontaneously. They lose freedom, in other words, and end up not doing very much except holding themselves together. They seem, then, to live less intensely than other persons. We can recognize them because of their apparent indifference, apathy, and lack of initiative. They are bored but it is the face of their adjustment to an inner problem, an unconscious defense related to nonspecific inhibitions.

There is also the boredom of the apathy that is a reaction to frustration. When persons experience frustration they can handle it in many ways. Withdrawing from the situation in order to isolate the self from stimulation is but one of these. They move back out of circulation where life cannot hurt them. It is something like being afflicted with a temporary paralysis, or holding one's breath so that one cannot feel the disappointment or pain involved in the situation.

We see this in another way in the obsessive-compulsive personality for whom joy and spontaneity are almost impossibly rare occurrences. They keep plodding along, putting the tiny jigsaw pieces of life together in order to contain their own inner anxiety, their heads bent down to the task that dehydrates them. They cannot enjoy life because they cannot afford to let themselves go. Their adjustment consists in a dull effort to get everything right and to keep it that way so that they will not suffer the feelings of guilt to which they would otherwise be vulnerable.

There is almost a cult of boredom among many young people. They believe that the stance of boredom in the face of life is the highest of human achievements. This failure to activate their enthusiasm for existence is demonstrated in their unwillingness to get involved, in their refusal to take on the risk of living. Coolness in the face of life may be supported by drugs which offer an alternate means of stimulation but which do not solve the root problem. Neither, of course, does alcohol. Indifference to existence impoverishes the personality, sentencing those who choose this pose to stand at the edges of the very experiences that could redeem them from the quicksand of boredom. They stay out of human relationships, saving themselves from the risks, but buying themselves boredom at the same time.

Boredom may also be considered a special form of communication. When we experience boredom in a certain situation it may be the message that somebody else is sending to us. Somebody else is boring us and that explains why we feel the way we do. We can, of course, send the same message to other people. It is an important signal to catch, whether we are the receivers or the senders. Experiencing boredom in this special way in any relationship is a clear sign that we need to trace its origins. Such boredom is not accidental. It is rather a powerful indication of some psychological dynamic to which we must direct our attention if we are interested in setting the relationship right again.

In the long run, we have our own responsibility for an interesting life. We literally have to give a damn and not just allow life to happen to us. This leads us to an important and central truth in relationship to our quite ordinary lives. While we may not have to seek the kind of ecstasy that is found in wars and in other violent experiences, we are not made to stay at the dead center of existence either. Our culture may be infected with too much talk about adjustment. There may be too many prescriptions written for too many tranquilizers. It is a sad day when our greatest passion is to stabilize and dull ourselves to the experience of life. Much of the how-to-do-it advice that we get points toward our better control of stress. Human beings are not, however, meant to float through life, bumping now and then off the sponge walls of a demystified existence. In order to be fully human we have to disrupt our adjustment constantly. We do this, not just for excitement, but for healthy purposes. It is in our nature to break out of static adjustments just as it is in our nature to outwit efficiency experts or institutions which try to take all the differences out of our personalities. Whenever we treat human beings like problems they manage to reassert their personalities anyway. They find their own way of doing things and they ignore all the instructions, architect's plans, or other notions that are provided for their control. That is part of the person's charm, part of the evidence we have for his inner resources to break out of boredom.

Persons are made to unbalance themselves, to sacrifice an achieved state of integration in view of achieving a higher and richer sense of their own wholeness. This is essential for creative activity and for creative living. It can happen in very ordinary circumstances and it is the best cure for boredom that we know. In the essence of the creative act, whether it is in carving a statue, writing a symphony, or composing a poem, artists must let go of themselves. They speak of learning "to throw themselves away" before they can achieve the integration that is represented in the work of art with which they are engaged. They must surrender their previous adjustment if they are going to do anything new. Artists do not want merely to repeat themselves. They are forever troubling themselves with a new and richer vision of the meaning of life and they try to share it with the rest of us. Inherent in this process is a purposeful unsettling of one's stable existence. This is not suicidal but rather a necessary step to greater growth. It is a kind of death the artist undergoes in order to achieve the experience of resurrection in and through art.

Just as the artist must undergo a certain surrender of a previous adjustment, so too do other persons in quite different circumstances. Persons do it, for example, on entering psychotherapy. They are willing to give up a previous adjustment—and neuroses are adjustments—in order to seek a better and more integrated way of living. This is painful and, as in physical illness when the body is rallying, the patient sometimes looks worse while in fact he or she is getting better. They reorganize themselves around a new vision of who they can be. They must, however, surrender something in the process.

This is what happens to people when they meet, fall in love, and decide to commit themselves to a relationship through life together. They have to give up their previous adjustments in order to grow together in a relationship in which the sharpening of their individuality will measure the strength of their mutuality. People do this when they enter a new profession, have to move to a new neighborhood, or even begin to make a new friend. We cannot stay the same and do any of these things successfully. We have to let go, learning "to throw ourselves away" in order to find a greater fullness in our own identity. We can all lead creative lives but the price is our willingness to die to what we have known and been comfortable with. Life is a succession of invitations to do exactly this even into old age. People who try to hold on to or merely look back toward the past miss the opportunity for an even richer and deeper definition of their own identity as the years pass. This works, as has been mentioned, in ordinary circumstances. It does not require great adventure, the discovery of a scientific wonder, or the sudden achievement of great popularity. It works in the simplest and the most common experiences of our everyday lives.

One of the charms of human beings is their distractability. That is a constant of life. They are forever searching their inner and outer environments in order to understand or discover what is new or possible. There would be no invention and no discovery without this characteristic of distractability in the lives of people. There would be no curious questions asked, no spirit of invention, no way of meeting someone new if we were not distractable. That is why we revolt against anything that we are supposed to do by rote. That is why, in fact, people are distracted at prayers which they recite by rote. What else can they do if they are truly human? Their best prayers flow, not from reading the same thing out of a book all the time, but out of entering into life in an open and honest way.

To live a creative life, even in ordinary circumstances, involves this tension at every level. To be creative we must live with contradictory experiences, that is, we have to balance the opposites that we discover in our personality and in our lives. We live with good and evil, with optimism and pessimism, with love and hate. We cannot be all one way if we are going to experience life in some depth. Life is boring for us unless we take the risks involved in letting ourselves feel the full dimensions of our human identities.

These observations are related to man's religious nature because these represent aspects of what it means to believe. Having faith is not the same as living in an unchanging and unchallenging environment. Nor is it saying yes to a static set of decrees or dogmas. It is something quite different. Believing is dynamic and creative and involves human beings in the process of dying and rising through their ordinary experiences all the time. Dynamic religion is essentially creative in the fact that it demands that people surrender something of themselves in order to reach out for an ever deeper identity. Faith is concerned always with the possibilities of life. It orients us to what we can yet become. It involves us with others through a commitment of our presence to what they themselves can become in life.

Belief involves us in a creative process that demands a surrender of an old adjustment in order to reach out to a new sense of ourselves. It requires us to do the same thing in order to make our energies available for the growth and development of others. We give back our possibilities to each other through believing in each other. This is a creative process that challenges the boredom of existence in a way that nothing else does. We are involved in an essentially religious experience when we are immersed in the ordinary tasks of life that require us to believe in ourselves and in each other. Our best energies are engaged and we discover also that the dynamic of death and resurrection is a constant reality rather than a remote abstraction in our lives. Boredom is a trophy of the superficial life. It is almost nonexistent in the lives of people who know how to look at themselves and at the world, who can still see how filled these are with possibilities, and who commit themselves, at great risk, to their realization every day.

13

The Trouble with Ourselves

A reasonably happy life depends to a large extent on whether we know, like, or can at least live with the truth about ourselves. For centuries preachers and other moralists have been scolding men and women for committing the terrible sin of pride. Pride, of course, consists of an overestimation of our abilities, in an inordinate sense of what we can accomplish completely on our own. Human beings have been beating their breasts and confessing this sin regularly for centuries seeking absolution for a fault hardly any of them ever committed. Pride is not now nor has it ever been the problem. The real trouble is that people do not have enough pride in themselves, that they do not believe enough in their own possibilities, that they feel bad rather than good about themselves and that they are unsure rather than overconfident in their own powers. The big trouble people have with themselves is based on an underestimation rather than an overestimation of who they are and what they can be.

Self-esteem is a problem that begins early with the way others react to us. Parents hold tremendous power in their hands to shape the child's sense of self. If they accept children as persons in their own right without demanding that they meet their own parental preconceptions or ideals, the children's chances of developing a healthy sense of themselves are enormously expanded. If, however, parents insist that children grow into their version of what they should be like and leave little room for individuality in their offspring, if they set conditions which the children must meet in order to be acceptable and loved, then the children have enormous trouble feeling comfortable with themselves throughout their lives. Reasonable self-esteem is a blessing rather than an accident. It is the outcome of living with people wise and self-acceptant enough to settle for us as we are, to respond to the truth of us, and to leave room enough for us to find who we really are without forcing us into any mold.

The power possessed by parents or by those who take their place in the raising of children is great because they can give or withhold love, the very thing we all need in order to develop into human beings. It is hard work to make up later in life for being made to feel consistently inferior all through infancy and childhood. Children who must learn ways of behaving that are not true to them to win parental affection are constantly engaged in collective bargaining for a basic emotional reward in life. Unfortunately, they never work out the right deal. There is always a catch in it, always some way that a question can be raised about their competence or about just what they would amount to if the loving parents did not support and sustain them. People who are not trusted find it very difficult to trust themselves; people who are not loved in and for themselves find it almost impossible to believe later on that somebody else could love them just as they are.

"I have never known what real love was," a person is liable to say and really mean it. They never knew what love was until they met somebody who accepted them without demanding that they change in order to prove their worth. It is an enlivening and enlarging experience that gives persons a sense of themselves which they never possessed before. This discovery of love later on in life is the best cure we know for the trouble of faulty self-esteem. People who do not believe in themselves sometimes hold themselves off from relationships, denying themselves the opportunity of finding someone who might accept and prize them in and for themselves.

Pride is certainly not the problem for people who cannot believe that others can see something worthwhile in them when they find it so difficult to find it for themselves. They may be preoccupied with a neurotic form of guilt or they may be crippled because they have never been accepted freely before. In any case, the achievement and preservation of self-esteem becomes a desperate and difficult battle for them. Without it their talents shrivel or are unused even though there is abundant evidence that they are indeed well endowed with talent.

Self-esteem is, in fact, a neglected commodity, especially in a country which values sexual performance as a source of self-identity. Actually, self-esteem is far more basic than sexual prowess, although the latter can be an important part of one's self regard. Nonetheless, self-esteem remains fundamental. If persons possess a reasonable and easy sense of their own truth and their own worth they find that they can handle the sexual aspect of their own experience far more easily. Sexuality does not become an enormous problem the way that it does for people who are unsure of themselves. The basic attitude toward the self, in other words, shapes the nature of the sexual response. If there is a failure of effectiveness as a result of a failure of self-confidence then the prophecy is self-fulfilling. Such failures, in many fields besides that of sexual performance, reinforce the person's sense of inadequacy. Such persons draw back to shield themselves from further scenes of embarrassment or shame. They do not feel worthy or able and they cut themselves off from the very sources of experience that might help them most in achieving a better sense of themselves and a happier and fuller life.

The difficulty for many people who experience shaky self-confidence is that of trying to find some combination of behaviors that will please others, win their favor, or, in some measure at least, get other people to like them. They cannot rely merely on what is true of their own personalities. So they depart from what is natural and easy for them and assume artificial roles designed to catch the prevailing winds and help them to greater social success. This introduces a false note, of course, that comes through in their relationships with others. Those around us pick it up when we are forced to put on an act or when we try to curry favor or merely display the opinions that seem to be current or popular. This is a multiplied danger in an era in which peer pressure is so enormous. Many young persons have a difficult time finding and believing in themselves because social approval depends on their achieving or producing the behavior that is generally accepted in their social set.

Young people feel the pressure of this peer approval intensely. Frequently they are forced by it to adopt and to exhibit attitudes and behaviors in which they do not themselves believe and which do not reflect or express their convictions or their personalities. They do this because social pressure is very potent and if young persons do not follow what the group believes they suffer ostracism and loneliness, bitter forms of rejection at a very vulnerable time in their lives. It is very difficult for many young people, who crave friendship and affection, to resist this influence. They want to be accepted, to be counted as those who are "in" with their fellows, and it is only a rare young person who feels strong and independent enough to stand aside from these pressures. Rejection would mean that they are on the outside of the world where they want to belong, that they fail where they most want to succeed, and their self-esteem is shattered, perhaps permanently as a result.

Peer pressure can bring young people to adopt attitudes that really muffle their own convictions. They feel, for example, that they must keep a strange code of silence and not turn in the drug dealers in their midst who may be damaging severely some of their friends. This is only one aspect of the kind of philosophy which, developed and propagated in the contemporary world, acquires the force of gospel among some good young people. They have to abide by it or be on the outside. This may, for example, force them to engage in premarital sex before they themselves even feel ready for it. There is a great deal of evidence to suggest that young people try to resist getting into sexual relationships when they understand that they are not themselves prepared for them. Sometimes the arrangements that look like young people living together are actually far less sexual when the behavior is closely examined rather than viewed from the outside. Such persons are meeting some kind of peer pressure demand but they are not following through with complete sexual activity.

The pressure of peer philosophical notions remains nonetheless strong. One, for example, that has had current favor is that "a person must do whatever his friend asks." This exudes a romantic aura and young people who try to live by it may feel that they are not only meeting the ideal of their groups but are also living in a highly noble way. No friendship, however, lasts very long when it is so lopsided. Such a notion is popular because it enhances the self-esteem of the person espousing it and seems to promise the rewards of friendship and love. People who do not make room for each other's individuality and who make such demands often end up tangled in a disappointing relationship from which they retreat wounded and unsure of themselves. Their self-esteem suffers greatly from trying to follow such a philosophy. It is clear that such a code has great advantages for partners who want to exploit their friends and who can exert strong pressure on them by reiterating the notion that good friends comply unfailingly to the wishes of the other.

Another variant of this was heard across campuses during the last several years and centered on respecting the freedom of one's friends even if they were using it to destroy themselves through excessive drinking and drug-taking. Even in religiously oriented institutions one could find people caught in the grip of this peer pressure philosophy. Instead of trying to help another person constructively they would let him or her go, building their case for this on the need to respect the freedom of the other even if the other is engaged in a slow kind of suicide. One cannot get mad at younger people for being caught in these attitudes. One can hope that they will find their way out of them while understanding why they accept them in the first place.

The big pressure comes from their need to be accepted by the group, to have the credentials of modern youth and, they hope, the emotional means to success and happiness.

These philosophies operate at all levels of life. We cannot accuse the young of having wrong ideas when frequently these ideas come from their elders in the first place. We often find adults caught in similar pressures, ready to do anything to win the approval and acceptance of their friends. What does a person do in the midst of such pressures with the threat of ostracism and loneliness as the only alternative? Not everybody is strong enough to withstand such forces; not everybody is blessed with a fair and loving childhood. What can we do about it?

We begin in the only place we can, by trying to establish a friendly relationship with ourselves. The beginning of friendship is not found in some magic in a person outside of us. It begins rather in the acceptance we give to ourselves, in the quiet and calm of facing and accepting who we are. The friendship we establish with ourselves becomes the model and pattern for all of our other friendships. If we fail at this, we are hampered severely in establishing relationships with others. If we want to know what our friendships are like, we need only take a look at our attitudes toward ourselves. We sometimes do not like to do this. It may be easier to look at our friendships and to find mirrored there our basic attitudes toward ourselves.

Are we uneasy, always trying to reassure friends or ourselves about our relationship with them? Are we suspicious or competitive? Do we feel guilty or do we seldom think about the needs of others? Do we call acquaintances friends even when our relationship is not deep enough to deserve this name?

We begin, in other words, not by trying to establish friendships outside of ourselves but by establishing one inside of ourselves. This is not an easy thing to do, especially if we have been living under the heavy penalty of being accepted only conditionally by parents or peers. It is hard to get beyond that and into our real selves, hard to find the gold that is really in us when we have been told repeatedly that we were mostly dross.

Establishing a friendly relationship with ourselves is the essence of being human to ourselves. We do it by redefining or clarifying our idea of ourselves. Psychologists refer to the self-concept as the characteristic way we look at ourselves and present ourselves to others. When we are healthy and reasonably in touch with ourselves our self-concept reflects us accurately. As mentioned in a previous chapter we have an idea of ourselves that matches the reality of ourselves. If, however, we have not been accepted or have had love doled out to us only if we have been able to meet certain conditions, then we may have a distorted self-concept, one that has filtered our interpretation of ourselves through the feedback we have received from other persons. What we see in ourselves is not really what is there but what we have been forced to see or what we have settled for seeing. Even when it is false we still act in and through this distorted self-concept. We present ourselves this way to the world. How do we get back in touch with the self of reality that lies beneath this?

Unless we are severely damaged in this regard and may require professional counseling, we can go a long way merely by listening more carefully to ourselves and to our own feelings. Through this we learn to accept ourselves, and so we loosen up our defenses so that we no longer have to hide from ourselves. When we do this we note the discrepancies between the way we have regarded ourselves and the way we really are. We can then put the world of the self back together in a truer and more enduring way. This takes time and patience as well as a readiness to be surprised and sometimes delighted by what we discover.

We must give ourselves permission to make this journey of self-discovery. We do that by lessening our own demands on ourselves, by giving ourselves as much of a break as we would be willing to give strangers struggling to discover the truth about themselves. We need to allow ourselves to live a little more freely, realizing that we are not going to do anything bad or dangerous if we do this. By respecting ourselves enough we give ourselves the room we need in order to get acquainted in an easy and reliable way with ourselves. We have to be ready to find that we are imperfect and not to be disturbed or distraught by this discovery. As we progress in our understanding of ourselves we find that we can live with our imperfections far more comfortably. We also do something else because when we have a truer sense of who we are we no longer hold up to ourselves an ideal that is well beyond us. We embrace the truth knowing that that is a secure base on which to build our lives. We design an ideal that is not an impossible dream, something we may never quite fully attain, but something we can reach for, stretching ourselves toward a deeper sense of ourselves.

We can also be prepared to find good things in the truth about ourselves. Most people hold back because they are afraid they are going to discover what is evil or bad. We may make discoveries of what is unfinished or imperfect but that does not mean we are going to find things that are impossible to look at or to accept about ourselves. Strangely enough we sometimes hide the best parts of ourselves, keeping them back from others because we are afraid they may reject them or laugh at them, finally estranging ourselves from our own best resources. Sometimes we hide our talents because we are afraid that if we admit them into light we will have to do something with them; we will have to change or use them, become more responsible and more adult.

We certainly don't hide the things that are bad about us. Everybody knows what is wrong with us and most people are not shy about telling us about our faults. There is an enormous amount of good that waits to be discovered in the lives of persons who are hesitant to trust themselves. These riches become the security they can count on as they develop a richer sense of themselves.

We can also ask ourselves what we are getting out of not taking a closer look at ourselves. What do we get out of being miserable? Are we merely trying to punish ourselves or do we honestly want to have a freer and better life? The latter is probably true of most of us but we may not be able to pursue this because we have not dealt with the reasons that make us hesitate, the little fears or uncertainties that make us delay in changing ourselves. We keep an uncomfortable version of ourselves because it is at least one with which we are familiar. What, we may well ask, are we waiting for? Do we live our lives as though we were expecting something bad to happen to us all the time?

That means it is time to begin, time to move into the sunlight and away from the shadows in which we only tremble about the bad possibilities of life. That is a small step but it takes us a long way toward a greater sense of satisfaction and self-esteem.

The automatic result of establishing a better friendship with ourselves is that we find that we have a better friendship with others. When we are freer in our relationships with our true selves we make the truth of ourselves more available to those around us. They find a more secure basis for a relationship with us. They discover that they like what is true about us and they respond more spontaneously to us. This is the kind of reinforcement that we need if we are going to have a deepened sense of our own worth. Just as a faulty sense of ourselves feeds on its own suspicions and uneasiness so a healthier sense of imperfect selves also nourishes and builds itself because it wins freely the regard of others. We are reinforced by those who love us. And people love us when we let them see the truth about ourselves. They are only uncertain when we are uncertain and faltering in our regard and respect for ourselves. They look at us freshly and are able to believe in us only as a consequence of our own work in discovering what we can believe in about ourselves.

14

A Lot of Little Troubles

Our biggest troubles are the ones that are bothering us at the moment. While we have indicated that our basic attitude toward our problems is decisive in handling them and delivering a sense of contentment and happiness to our lives, it is worth examining some of the ordinary troubles that crop up regularly. These may be the in-between time troubles, the ones that are always there in one way or another, sometimes muted and sometimes, especially when we are relatively free of more serious troubles, more demanding of our attention. None can be solved unless we look back at our basic attitudes toward ourselves and life. They include such things as:

Money

Money is a trouble when we don't have it, a trouble when we want it, and a trouble when we finally get it. It has caused more mischief in marriage and family life, ended more friendships, and generated more frustration than any other factor in history.

It is not quite true to say that people will do anything for money. They will do plenty, however, especially when other arguments fail. What it costs frequently decides what is done, even when nobler motives are supposedly involved in projects of one kind or another. It is sad but true that we have to deal with money whether we like it or not and that the management of our finances is a significant element in our total experience of life.

Even those who take a vow of poverty should have some idea of the value of money. Money is not intrinsically evil. One must be fairly well subsidized by generous people in order to live a life of poverty. Those who do not have money find it very easy to make judgments about the way people with money should spend it. So we all of us, those who have it and those who don't, need to think about our attitudes toward money. It is wonderful to be free of the care of money. But nobody really is. Even if one is vowed to poverty as true as that of St. Francis one must have a concern for the value of things, and one must be ready to see the psychological importance of money. It is not an unfortunate and unnecessary trouble in life. It does reflect value in a certain way. As, for example, when it tells what our daily work is truly worth it can be a just judgment on our ability and our energies. Whenever we use things, no matter who paid for them, we tell something about our attitude toward money. We ought to pay attention to the messages if we are going to lead adult lives.

Much of the trouble connected with money, of course, comes from its absence when we need it. There are those who have become "credaholics" in the United States, getting themselves far over their heads in debt, paying a little bit for everything each week, but never getting out of the red. It is easy to overspend in a consumer's society that is full of enticements. It takes some discipline, some search of the self in advance, to be able to plan the wise use of whatever money we have. A married couple who are not able to discuss and agree on what is a sensible standard of living for them before they live together are sentencing themselves to one endless trouble that can finally break their marriage apart. It is not the things that we talk about that cause trouble; it is usually the things we do not talk about, and money is one of them. People take a lot for granted, assuming that each understands the other's viewpoint, and it is only at showdown time or, as the phrase goes, when we reach the bottom line, that the ugly truths come out. These are followed by accusations and recriminations and then by the dizzying spin of a relationship plummeting toward earth.

Money is trouble that we can anticipate. We know the figures and we know the facts. If we can't keep within a budget or within some realistic plan of investments, then we have to go beyond logic and investigate our psychology. What is there about us that needs to spend money, perhaps, or what are we doing if we live perilously close to financial disaster all the time? These are questions individuals must answer for themselves but they are questions that they don't even like to ask. It is also possible for people to be too saving, to hold on to everything for fear that the worst is about to occur, and to end up deprived of the decent things that hard-earned money can buy. The troubles with money can be anticipated and they should be discussed in advance because they cannot be left to whim or to chance. We are the authors of our own financial policies and we cannot blame anybody else for the judgments we make in this regard. We can avoid a good deal of trouble if we use common sense coupled with a realistic understanding of our own position in life. We also transmit something to our children or students through our attitudes toward money and possessions. They learn subtly but powerfully what value we put on it, what energies we put into its acquisition, and what kind of judgment we use in spending it. Money isn't everything but it certainly is something that says a lot about who we are and what kind of lives we lead.

Liberation

Liberation is not just for women, although it has been discussed in regard to them far more than in regard to men. Men, however, need liberation as much as women. The movement toward greater human realization will continue strongly over the next generation. Women's Lib is not just a topic to talk about, nor just a political trouble that will soon pass away. It raises an important issue to which all of us must give our attention. Being a liberated person does not mean being totally free of constraints. It refers rather to the persons who understand something of the reality of their own human nature and who are not trapped by some distorted image of themselves.

Being human to ourselves is based on a mature sense of the possibilities of the human situation. It means we are trying to be men and women capable of experiencing life in a rich and significant way. It suggests that we are not going to be the victims of prejudice, old wives' tales, or fears of each other in pursuing this goal. The goal may not be achieved for many generations but each of us is committed to examining our lives in order to stake a claim on the freedom that we need to become truly ourselves. This includes living in a world that does have restraints, limitations, and loose ends. We are liberated in an imperfect world and not even liberation makes us perfect. It makes us more fully human and more capable of understanding our experience of existence.

Relatives

Everything is relative, they say, and if you have a house in the country you find out how true that is. One can be all for the values of the extended family without living an in-law-ridden existence. Everybody cannot be involved in everybody else's business all the time. This, however, is one of the troubles that arises when people do not maintain a healthy independence from their original family and from their other relatives. It is in relationship to our relatives, all of whom we want to love and from whom we expect the same, that we can become so ensnarled that we end up never having a life of our own. It is in working out an adult manner of relationship with our relatives that we achieve a balance between independence and dependency, between what is healthy in both of these experiences. This is not a matter that takes care of itself.

That is why distance lends enchantment. We can see our relatives better when we are just a little way off from them, far better than when we are staring down each other's throats all the time. We have to have a balanced approach to living with our relatives in order to spare ourselves the unnecessary trouble that comes when we are tangled in each other's affairs all the time. When we cannot have physical distance we can be mindful enough of its need to establish some psychological distance. We can avoid making some of the mistakes, like lending money to relatives without a written agreement, which almost always end in disaster.

Good relatives are essential to a sense of ourselves and to our appreciation of our traditions. We belong to the same clan. We reflect something of a distinct and respectable religious and ethnic strain. We derive much support from closeness to those who share our own deep convictions about religion, race, and other significant issues of life. We should remember, however, that most murders occur between people who know each other and frequently between family members. Let the weather get hot, the irritations grow more intense, and the mayhem can begin. This is not what happens in most families, of course, but the strained feelings, the taut nerves, and the vague wonder about how we got into all this—these are familiar to anybody who has been overdosed by relatives at any time.

Our most sensible approach is to locate the trouble spots, such as money and varied opinions about the way each other's children should be raised, and to avoid the situations in which these topics are likely to come up. It is something like the old occasion of sin. Here, however, it is avoiding the occasion of the famous family squabble. People have to be awfully sure of each other and of their tolerance for each other's oddities, for example, to plan and take a vacation together. That is a test of what is truest and best in all people. Each person must search his or her own life situation to identify those points of pressure in family life. We can do a lot just by avoiding the topics and places that are sure to result in friction. Family trouble is always there, one way or another, but with some intelligence we can avoid a great deal of it that is unnecessary.

We can pick our friends but we can't pick our relatives. That is a truth that can never be undone. One walks prudently and decides slowly in order to preserve what is rich and full of love in a family setting. It is hard and practical work, however, rather than the romantic forays in mild estrangement that one sees in programs like "The Waltons" or the "Little House on the Prairie." Keeping close to and yet separate from one's family is the key to avoiding some of life's most unnecessary troubles.

Neighbors

In a world of high rises and suburbs without sidewalks it is possible for many people who live close to each other never to know each other. That is a twentieth-century phenomenon that has led to a great deal of isolation and loneliness. It has made families turn toward themselves to secure the emotional sustenance they need for life. But neighbors are there, people to get to know as friends with whom we fashion a community that is humanly necessary to sustain and nourish us in life. The family that depends only on itself may survive but at a great emotional cost. A family that has friends in its neighbors multiplies its opportunities for personal growth and for emotional support.

People have a lot of trouble, in other words, if they do not work at developing a network of friends. Sometimes these do not come from the physical neighborhood but rather arise out of relationships in business or in a profession. In a highly mobile society in which communications are abundant and instantaneous, people can constitute a community together even though they are not physically in the same neighborhood. In any case, the drive to develop relationships that have the signs of true friendship about them is significant evidence of our humanity. We do need each other and we cannot survive the big troubles of life if we only have acquaintances.

We can also avoid a lot of trouble if we follow common sense in dealing with our territorial neighbors. People who live near each other, whether it is in apartments or on the same street, need to respect each other and each other's property rights. There is something basic in human nature that is connected with a person's sense of what constitutes his own "turf." Everybody stakes out their own life space and being a sensible neighbor is built on understanding this. We cannot violate each other's life space—in this case, each other's territory—without delivering a message about our irreverence for each other. Nothing builds bad feelings more quickly than neighbors who have not understood this primary law of getting along with each other. Good fences, as the saying goes, build good neighbors. Fences, however, are more often built because neighbors have failed to get along very well without them. Many a fence has been built in spite, a last symbol of relationship that may have been needlessly destroyed by insensitivity.

We avoid a lot of trouble getting along with others if we learn early in life to make allowances for the fact that we will all offend each other periodically. We may do it just as much as the average neighbor or close friend does it to us. We offend largely as a result of insensitivity, because we fail to recognize just how important some event, opinion, or truth is to somebody else. It is easy to offend people; sometimes people are offended when they should not be. Friendship is a powder-filled room, however, and we can enter it and, while striking a match to find our way, cause a good deal of mischief. Common sense in this regard is extraordinarily helpful.

We can hearken back to some of the oldest and the longest-running adages of the English language. Counting ten, for example, before we say something when we are upset is one of the best ways to avoid unnecessary trouble with friends and neighbors. The best version of this, actually, tells us that when we are really irritated we shouldn't say what we are tempted to say at all. This is particularly true when, as is often the case, we have let some situation grow worse by ignoring it or by failing to say something when we have the opportunity. It is also true when we have a friend or neighbor who may be under tension or may be giving signals of being a little peculiar or bizarre. We need to pause and step back and calculate just what effect losing our temper would have in any of these situations.

Our best approach to getting along well with those with whom we rub elbows all the time is to try to discuss, early and gently, those areas that we find irritating. It is much better to bring difficult subjects up before they are major occasions for estrangement. We can all inspect our lives and see the price we have paid for putting off quiet discussions about touchy issues. When we don't do this we are mad both at the neighbor, or the friend, and ourself and our resentment builds until we react harshly, doing more harm than good and perhaps irreparably damaging our friendship. It is only common sense to do this. If we find that we put off discussing the sources of irritation with those we want to keep as friends we need to examine our reluctance. We make victims of ourselves when we fail to act in this regard.

Everything Is Bad For You

Sooner or later we realize that almost everything, if taken in the wrong measure, is bad for us. New revelations are made every day about the evils of almost everything we eat, drink, touch, or even look at. What are we going to do about this long list of troubles that include dirty pictures, drinking, and drugs?

First we need to examine our own attitudes. We may find that we do not have any attitudes that we could truly call our own, that we have, in fact, been operating from a series of dimly held prejudices or impressions and that we have not thought through our position on some of these issues. It is difficult to sift through the conflicting reports or opinions on subjects like these. Doing this, however, is one of the mature and maturing activities of life. We liberate ourselves, breaking out of our own prejudices by both broadening and deepening our appreciation of life, through thinking through these attitudes. We may have to deal with our own conflicts as we sort out what we believe in about these areas in order to discover why we believe the way we do. Our own personal familial experience may have shaped the attitudes by which we now live or which we hand on to others.

Nothing replaces good judgment in any one of these areas. Recent studies about drinking, however, reveal that Americans have strange and uneasy conflicts about drinking. A great many people are ready to denounce alcohol but hardly any of them want anybody to interfere with their own individual drinking habits. It is very easy for people to be moralistic and judgmental in any one of these areas. This generally leads to their making things worse instead of better. That is generally what happens when we have not worked out our own conflicts and end up acting them out in our relationships instead.

Many persons do not like excessive drinkers and tend to perceive them as individuals who deliberately and consciously choose the punishing existence of alcoholism. We may stand aloof from them, feeling that it is their own fault, and that they have to pull themselves up by themselves. In a recent report from the *National Institute of Alcohol Abuse,* Dr. Morris Chafetz explores many of the attitudes of contemporary Americans toward the problem of alcohol. He says that alcoholism is a treatable illness but that our attitudes toward it seem in conflict and therefore impede our national and individual readiness to do something about it in our own families and in our own lives. Alcoholism is a treatable illness but different treatments are required by different individuals. Early identification is vital if we are to help people to deal with and survive successfully this terrible difficulty. It is a mistake here, as in other situations, to delay or put off discussing or doing something about the things that are difficult or touchy. Many people know that their co-worker is a heavy drinker but choose to cover up rather than help the individual to get some kind of needed assistance at a time when it is important. This is also true among young people as well as among older people.

The most critical ages for the epidemic problem of alcoholism in the United States are between eighteen and twenty. Is this a trouble we leave to other agencies or people, one we discount or look away from in our own experience, one we may hesitate to do anything about even in our own lives? We have to ask, for example, what climate we create in our own homes about the use or abuse of alcohol. Is it funny to be drunk? Is it still something to boast about? Are we inconsistent in our use of alcohol and our attitudes toward the use of alcohol by others? We don't have to be alcoholics to be inconsistent and therefore confusing in the kind of education we hand on to those closest to us.

Common sense tells us that a sensitive regard for those we love would lead us to identify the symptoms of excessive drinking early and to try to do something constructive to assist those in whom we see these signs. It may be a difficult thing to walk the line between being constructively and humanly helpful and falling into the danger of being a clumsy do-gooder. We save a lot of trouble when we are willing to take that risk. What we do about drinking in our own lives—and that depends on whether we have thought through our attitudes on the problem—decides whether we are going to have trouble with this or not.

Pornography

Pornography is obviously a trouble in contemporary America. It is also a fact of life that is not going to go away. It has survived through the centuries, perhaps because we have been unwilling to resolve our attitudes toward it, just as we have been hesitant to resolve them about alcohol. Here again there is no substitute for maturity and good judgment. In the long run, despite whatever campaigns or other urgings are present *pro* or *con* about pornography, the matter is only handled well by good people who are able to make up their own minds about the meaning of pornography. We need not burn books, or, on the other hand, trivialize freedom of speech by defending the rights of sleazy pornographers as though this were the only liberal cause on the continent. We could lessen this trouble considerably by removing some of the drama that has been associated with it. Pornography is not the scourge of all time and if we cut it down to its proper size, neither glorifying it nor condemning it outlandishly, it would be far less troublesome to all of us.

Our concern should be to build the values and character that enable persons to make good judgments about the taste and moral quality of pornography. That means that our best response to the trouble of pornography lies in creating the environment in which healthy human persons can grow. The healthier we make the environment, the less troublesome the whole issue will become.

We may have to examine our own attitudes here, however, to discover whether we have even thought them through. Is sex a subject we still refuse to talk about seriously? Many people talk about it but not many talk about it seriously. In general—as is exemplified on many television talk shows—there is a rather adolescent manner of dealing with sexuality that prevails in the lives of many adults. Can we discuss sex calmly and without leering or being overly moralistic? Sexuality suffers from underdiscussion despite the abundance of information about it that has come to us in recent years. It also suffers from overdiscussion by those crusaders who want to turn back the clock and by those super-liberal persons who think they are responding to the questions of the young when they are really talking about the doubts of their own middle age.

Pornography is only one aspect of our overall attitude toward human personality. If we treat ourselves humanly—giving ourselves room enough to grow and to make good judgments for ourselves—we avoid much of the trouble that goes with last-minute repression of the symptoms of unresolved sexual problems. We have to contribute to the general maturing of the population in regard to sexuality or we will contribute in some way to the deepening of the problem. If pornography and sexuality are still excessively troublesome to us then our first step is to do something about ourselves so that we can be rid of prejudices, emotional entanglements, and rumors about the subject. The more we stand clear of these the better we are going to assist all of those, children and students and friends, who are close to us in life.

Drugs

How many times can we issue a call for common sense? Unleashed wrath doesn't settle much and it hasn't convinced anybody, especially in regard to the use of drugs in contemporary society. This goes especially for the "soft" drugs such as marijuana, the values or dangers of which continue to be debated even by the scientific community. We need to be informed on these issues and, once again, we need to think through our own position and stick to it. The trouble is that many persons have no position at all. One of the problems that has always hindered the moral development of the young is the inability of adults to hold clear and consistent positions on important issues in life. Some super-liberal people have been crushed by the fact that young people have ended up losing respect for them precisely because they were so willing to let the young make up their own minds on vital questions such as taking drugs, religion, and sexuality.

We can reassure ourselves that there is nothing wrong with stating our mature convictions—if they are our mature convictions. Through these we establish the limits within which we choose to live and which we expect to be effective and appropriate in the lives of those for whom we have any special responsibility. There is nothing to be ashamed about in having a conviction, even if it sounds old-fashioned. We state the things we live by, the principles that define who we are, the signals that give evidence of the fact that we have dealt in some depth with these issues and have made decisions about the direction of our own lives.

We know that it is difficult to help others develop self-control merely by insisting on excessive authoritarian control over their own lives. We do not help others to develop self-control by leaving it all up to them either. They need to feel the presence and influence of people who have thought through the important issues of existence honestly.

We would save a lot of trouble in most of the areas of life if we were clearer about our own values and goals. Are we willing to run the risk of having others dislike us? This getting others to like us often becomes the all-important goal and it interferes with people ever discovering or stating their own principles about human life. A great deal of trouble can be saved if we work at a position that we can truly identify as our own and stick to it, without rancor or fear, on any of these issues.

Despite all this, we will never get it all together. We will always be caught up in the puzzle and the mystery of life itself. It is filled with troubles all the time and we make our way through it only if we are willing to work at it steadily and fairly. We work out our salvation and find happiness not by avoiding troubles but by working them through with as much integrity as we can.

